THE
FIELDS IN
WINTER

THE
FIELDS IN WINTER

GRAHAM DOWNING

With photographs by the writer
and illustrations by Marianne Downing
and Jonathan Yule

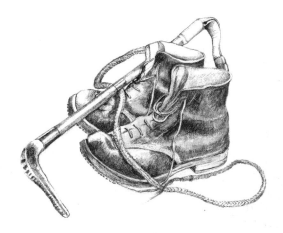

DAVID & CHARLES
Newton Abbot   London

To Ronnie

All photographs by the author except the following:
Anglia T.V. p83; Nigel Broom pp9, 181, 183;
John Darling pp110 (inset), 149; P. H. Emerson
pp12, 15, 20-1, 28, 54-5, 73; Grafton Country Pictures
pp8, 165, 186; Dick Makin pp25, 110 (main picture),
179; Shooting Times p93.
    Other illustrations by Marianne Downing except
pp98-9 by Jonathan Yule.

British Library Cataloguing in Publication Data
Downing, Graham
    The fields in winter: sporting memories of a bygone age.
    1. Great Britain. Field sports, history
    I. Title
    799.0941
    ISBN 0-7153-9432-0

Typeset by ABM Typographics Ltd, Hull
and printed in Italy by New Interlitho SpA., Milan
for David & Charles Publishers plc
Brunel House   Newton Abbot   Devon

CONTENTS

FOREWORD

It is said that the countryside is a state of mind; that it exists not so much in the fields, woods and hedgerows as in the attitudes of those who live amongst them. There is a good deal of truth in that assertion. The popular conception of rural Britain is still one of pretty villages of thatch and timber, of mellow stone churches, winding lanes and high hedgebanks. But when those pink-washed cottages are little more than a dormitory for the nearest city, when beyond each neatly manicured hedge and gravelled drive lurks a BMW or a swimming pool, then one starts to wonder just how much of the rural idyll we see around us or visit fleetingly at weekends is anything more than a romantic façade. Urban influences and values now extend so far beyond the suburbs that much of village Britain shares far greater cultural affinity with the city than with its own rural past.

The true countryside is in the heart of the countryman, one whose way of life and whose thinking is attuned to the land and the changing seasons, and traditionally one whose living is rooted in farm and forest or amongst the local community itself. In the closing years of the twentieth century the real countryman is a dwindling species.

Many more of us have a dash of the countryman within ourselves, however, and that goes especially for those who participate in traditional field sports such as shooting or hunting. For the field sportsman the countryside is not merely a place in which his recreation takes place – that much could be said for the golfer or the cross-country runner – it is an integral part of his sport, just as he, the hunter or the shooter, is an extension of the countryside itself; a living piece of the rural sub-culture, part of the landscape.

Man has been a hunter ever since he learned to stand on his hind legs. Long before he ever became a farmer he pursued the birds, beasts and fishes to provide food for himself and his family. The need to hunt is something which runs deep within all of us, and although that need is nowadays sublimated in a variety of ways – in sport or in business, for example – there are still millions of people throughout the developed world who hunt, shoot or fish not because they have to, but for the pleasure and fulfilment which hunting, shooting and fishing bring.

A recent survey into the attitudes of those who take part in sporting shooting indicated that while the most frequently expressed reason for shooting was the enjoyment of the countryside, fascination with the hunt itself came not far behind and was listed by around half of the respondents.

Field sports, therefore, still supply an important need in modern man, although there are those who would argue that civilisation and the moral and spiritual progress of mankind has rendered that need redundant. To them I would say that it is civilisation which has mutated: field sports remain as a sheet anchor, a means by which we can clear our minds of the complexities of modern living and return, however briefly, to simpler, purer values.

There are, of course, those whose lives have been affected only modestly by the twentieth century. Those whose attitudes and experience have been shaped by the natural rhythms of the countryside rather than the vagaries of the oil market or the *Financial Times* Index. Those whose knowledge of wild plants and creatures was not acquired from books or college lecturers but absorbed by a natural osmosis from the cradle onwards. Field sports have bred and shaped many such people, but none more so than those whose professional lives have been devoted to hunting, shooting and fishing in all its various complex guises. If there is a true culture of rural Britain then it is to be found amongst the gamekeepers, huntsmen, harbourers, warreners and their like, men whose entire working existence has been spent amongst the fields in winter.

Their balanced attitudes to life hold so many lessons for the rest of us, lessons which they themselves have learned from patient observation and hard-won experience, valuable lessons which are not shared lightly with others. For this reason, if for no other, the countryman's story is one worth listening to.

It has been my privilege in researching and writing this book to meet and talk to many such people. Some of them I have known since boyhood and from them I have learned much about the ways of wild birds and creatures; others are of more recent acquaintance. Some are mentioned by name within these pages, while others are present only by way of their tales and reminiscences which are blended in amongst some stories of my own. But to all of them I owe a debt of gratitude.

My thanks go also to those who have given other practical help towards this book: to the friends who have welcomed me into their homes whilst I travelled with pen and camera, and more especially to my wife, Ronnie, to whom this book is dedicated and who has provided her constant support and encouragement. Particular thanks are due to my mother, who worked tirelessly on the illustrations – both the pencil sketches, the pen-and-ink drawings and the beautiful paintings of fruits, flowers and fungi – and also, finally, to Jonathan Yule for his evocative watercolour of punt gunning and the atmospheric pictures which he has produced for the dust jacket.

Graham Downing
Nayland, 1990

HEREWARD'S HEIR

When Ernie James was a young man in the 1920's
there were literally dozens like him; men whose lives
were worked out to the whisper of reeds in a keen east
wind, the glow of a thousand golden dawns across the
flooded fen, the whicker of duck wings and the boom
of the punt gun.

LEFT AND ABOVE
The washes in summer

Tucked into the shelter of the Old Bedford bank as it cuts its twenty mile course through the heart of the fens nestles Plover Cottage in the village of Welney. Small, neat and whitewashed, it is the sort of place where you might expect to see carefully clipped rose bushes and tidy lawns. Instead, the gnarled apple trees are hung with drying eel nets, while boathooks, poles, eel boxes and an old upturned punt mark this out as the home of Ernie James, eel catcher, wildfowler and all-round fenman.

Now well into his eighties, Ernie is among the last of a dying breed. When he was a young man in the 1920s there were literally dozens like him throughout the fens, men who made their living from the watery wilderness. Today their names are still half-remembered by the older generation of fen folk – Will Kent, Joey Butcher, Cutty See the skater, the legendary Hagan Smart. These were the 'Fen Tigers', rough, tough men whose lives were worked out to the whisper of reeds in a keen east wind, the glow of a thousand golden dawns across the flooded fen, the whicker of duck wings and the boom of the punt gun. They were heirs to a tradition stretching down the centuries from the days of Hereward the Wake.

It is hard now to visualise the sort of close-knit communities which existed in the fens of Ernie's youth, communities which wrested a living from the land and water about them, men and women who led isolated lives, attuned to the rhythm of the seasons. In those days the fens were wilder than they are now. Where boundless fields of winter wheat bend in the breeze, or sugar beet and celery wax fat in the rich earth, once there grew nothing but reeds and sedge in the quaking mire. Fish without number swam in the fenland rivers and in winter the skies were darkened by the wings of wildfowl.

Each product of the fen featured in the local economy, for the old fenmen had no regular jobs. In the spring, when the eels ran upstream on moonlit nights, it was time to set nets and traps woven to ancient pattern from willow wands. Ernie's eel hives, four feet long and baited with worms threaded onto copper wire, sometimes yielded a stone of eels in a night. I must say that when I used them as a boy on the Norfolk broads I never managed to achieve such weighty catches. A handful of wriggling eels was the most that I could ever expect, but oh! what excitement there was when the hive was dragged out of the water on a misty May morning, its wooden bung removed and the contents tipped eagerly into an old hessian sack!

But then of course Ernie's own hives were set with the skill of a master eel catcher who knew every trick; every nook and hollow under the bank where the eels like to lie along the lilied waters of the Old Bedford River. 'I like to set my hives under the roots of an ol' willow, 'cos the eels, they like to suck the bark of the willows, you know.'

Ernie James making a traditional fenland eel hive. LEFT: Stripping the willows

And there was no simple sack for Ernie – he used great wooden chests, drilled all over with holes and sunk into the river so that the eels could be kept alive and fresh for market.

In summer the weedy dykes were cut laboriously by hand and marsh litter was

harvested to supply bedding for horses. There were mole traps to be set along the marsh banks, for the fenland river walls are particularly vulnerable to the tunnelling activities of moles, and the smallest leak could result in the inundation of a thousand rich acres. Then there was the osier harvest, when great bundles of willow wands were cut for basket-making and the village girls chattered and gossiped as they stripped the bark from the green-skinned withies.

In the winter came floods and frost. When the fenland rivers froze over and the ice was strong enough to bear the weight of a man, then the thoughts of the Fen Tiger turned to skating. Not fancy shilly-shallying around on the ice, but hard-bitten racing for cash prizes. Big money was there to be won by the best fen skaters, with purses put up by the local farmers who sponsored their own champions as though they were bare-fisted prize fighters. And winter was the season which Ernie James loved the most, for it was the time for plover netting and wildfowling. 'Gunning and plover catching were always what I liked to come round first,' he reminisces.

Ernie's fowling grounds were but a gun-shot away from his own front room. Walk

Willows were grown to supply the local basket-maker. LEFT: Wildfowling on the Hundred Foot washes

out of the side door of Plover Cottage, up a flight of rough-hewn steps, and you find yourself on the bank of the Old Bedford River. Unhitch the punt from its mooring in the reeds and after a few short strokes of the pole you climb the far bank to enter the magical world of the Hundred Foot washes.

After the drear browns and greys of the arable fenland farms, the washes come as something of a shock. Here, sandwiched between the Delph and the Hundred Foot rivers is a pencil of green and silver, three quarters of a mile wide and twenty miles long, cutting through the heart of the fens. Throughout the summer months the cattle stand hock deep in the rich grazing for which the washes are famous, but when the winter floods are up the vista is one of short-cropped turf, rushes bleached almost white in the keen wind, and great glistening sheets of floodwater out of which lean drunken gate posts under an all-embracing sky. It is a stark and uncompromising landscape, but possessed of a haunting beauty. And all about are the countless flocks of wildfowl: mallard and teal in their thousands and wigeon in their tens of thousands, lifting, turning, wheeling against the winter cloudscape, filling the air with their whistling cries.

In fact the washes are a product of the seventeenth-century drainage schemes of the Dutchman Cornelius Vermuyden. With a number of ambitious drainage projects already under his belt, and with the blessing of King Charles I, Vermuyden drove his ruler-straight drainage rivers across the fenland landscape, cutting off a great bend in the River Ouse. Between the rivers, the Hundred Foot washes acted as a sump, taking the overflow when the winter floodwaters from half of the east Midlands became too much for the narrow river channels.

And they continue to do so today, flooding in the winter and becoming a haven for wildfowl and wildfowlers alike. In Ernie's day the gunners were professionals, shooting for the market. They shot from gunning punts; not the costly, custom-designed punts of the gentlemen wildfowlers, but undecked workaday craft, slab-sided and armed with a great muzzle-loading punt gun, often of unknown ancestry and owing more to the village blacksmith than the city gunmaker. Today, one of the last gunning punts to have worked the washes sits in the somewhat incongruous surroundings of Welney Wildfowl Refuge. Punt and gun, 'Bacca Jack', belonged to Josh Scott, who was himself a professional wildfowler before he became warden at the refuge.

'I used a flintlock when I first started,' says Ernie. 'When we wanted to change over to percussion locks, the old blacksmith used to alter 'em, but I don't think breech loaders are any better than the old muzzle loaders. You might only get one shot in a day, so that makes no difference you being able to load her up again in a hurry.' And he recalls, 'I've had thirteen punt guns through my hands plus a few four bores.'

Two of those guns I know well. One, a monstrous great thing with a bore of an inch and three quarters, hangs on the wall of my family home in Norfolk. It is fitted with a crudely carved stock, hacked from a baulk of oak, held onto the massive barrel with two jubilee clips. The simple dog-lock, driven by an exposed coil spring, must have been fashioned in some fenland forge amongst the ploughshares and the horseshoes. An unassuming, utterly utilitarian sort of fowling piece but, as they say in Welney, 'She do goo, bor'. Go she most certainly does, and I bet that old gun has killed some birds in its time.

The other of Ernie's punt guns with which I am intimately familiar hangs in my own gunroom. She is a muzzle loader, nine feet long, sleek and grey painted. When loaded with three ounces of coarse-grained black gunpowder, an oakum wad and three quarters of a pound of shot, she shoots tight and true, sounding off with a roar like the crack of doom followed by a cloud of white smoke. The gun, like so many of the old punt guns, was originally a flintlock, but she was converted years ago to the more convenient percussion ignition system, a nipple to take the copper percussion cap being simply welded onto the cover of the exposed flash pan.

'She belonged to old Mr Dewsbury at Oxlode,' Ernie explained to me as he recounted the history of the ancient gun. 'There were two Dewsburys as used to go gunning, one time o' day. One had a wooden leg that he used to take off when he climbed into his punt, and I bought the gun off his widow. Albert Smart – that's old Hagan Smart's nephew – put that stock on, sixty years ago now,' he adds, pointing to the squared, squat oaken butt, designed to be braced against the thwarts of an open gunning punt.

The Dewsbury gun was much admired and coveted by the Welney gunners, for it threw a dense pattern of shot which would scythe right through a pack of unsuspecting wigeon. Will Kent, the man who taught Ernie James much of his wildfowling, once offered his best cow for the gun, but old Dewsbury was a canny fellow and was not to be tempted by such blandishments. He wouldn't part with it, and kept the gun until his death.

Will and his wife lived in a tiny cottage that stood virtually on the washes – its parlour would flood during most winters. I knew the house well when I first started shooting at Welney, for it was tucked away in a little wood which we would walk past at daybreak on our way to morning flight. The place was alive with rabbits, and there was always a marvellous pigeon flight out of the trees at sunrise, for the woodpigeons used Will Kent's spinney as a favourite roost.

They still do, but sadly the cottage is no more. Its weatherboarded and pantiled structure, weakened and rotted with the floods of ages, was dilapidated enough when I first knew it, and it was not long before time and weather did their worst. Now the cottage is just a memory, and the site on which it stood belongs to the RSPB.

Will Kent was one of half a dozen fowlers, each of whom had his own 'territory'. 'Before I started there were the Peppers, the Smarts, the Scotts, Cutty See and Will Kent. I learned my gunning off him, but I killed a sight more ducks than he ever did. When he packed up I took over his patch,' recalls Ernie.

In summer the land was grazed by its owners, the local farmers, but once the winter floods were up the gunners would, by traditional right, go anywhere they chose, though each within his own jealously guarded territory. Each gunner's stretch of wash measured about a mile in length, and woe betide anyone who strayed onto the fowling grounds of his neighbour.

These local demarcation lines were not dictated solely by rivalry, however; they had their practical point when men stalked ducks with punt guns. 'There was one time when two of the Kents were stalking up among a load of thistles. I was watching them from the bank and they both came up against the same lot of birds without knowing it. They were both just about to fire when the birds got up, and I reckon that's a good job they did too, or someone would have got a bit o' lead in 'em.' A risky business, was punt gunning on the washes.

There was danger, too, from the ancient hammer guns which were carried in the punts as 'cripple stoppers' to deal with any birds not killed outright by the discharge of the big gun. 'I was shooting one Boxing Day, and snatched the hammer gun off the gun beam. Well, I'm darned if that didn't blow a hole through the bottom of the boat!'

The punts which the wash gunners used were around sixteen or seventeen feet long, pointed at stem and stern and painted light grey, a colour which renders a boat almost invisible once it is on the water beneath a bleak winter sky. They were built to be worked singlehanded, were undecked and open to all weather, unlike the much more sophisticated punts which were designed and built for coastal shooting by gentlemen gunners such as the great Sir Ralph Payne-Gallwey. Sir Ralph set the seal on sporting punt design at the end of the last century, and his plans are still used today.

Across the punt, just forward of its widest point, was a thwart where the stock of the big gun would rest, its muzzle tucked into the stem of the boat. With the lighter guns it was possible to absorb the recoil through a wooden board, something akin to a bootjack, one end of which fitted around the stock of the gun whilst the other was pressed against the floor of the punt. Some beefy wildfowlers even bore the kick of the gun against the shoulder, suitably padded with a sack of straw. But for any punt gun firing a reasonable charge of eight ounces or more, it was necessary to use a breeching rope, attached to the gun through a hole in the stock or by means of trunnions fixed to the barrel. The rope was then made secure to the punt so that the boat itself would absorb the recoil of the big gun.

Behind the gun would lie the fowler, his kit beside him in the boat, contained in a 'budget' made of cowhide, stitched together with copper wire and fitted with a wooden base. Such a budget is a remarkably waterproof container, and will fulfil the vital function of keeping dry both the powder for the big gun and the priming caps. Also in the budget would be the powder and shot measures, carefully made from cow horns and carved to throw exactly the right charge for each individual gun.

When there were ducks ahead of him, the gunner would get down out of sight behind the gun and work the punt forwards using a pair of hand paddles with blades about two-and-a-half inches wide by fourteen inches long. He would attach the paddles to the sides of the punt with thin cord, so that when the time came to fire the big gun, normally from a range of around sixty to seventy yards, it was simply a matter of lining up on the ducks, dropping the paddles and pulling the lanyard which was fixed to the gun's trigger mechanism. There was no aiming system for the punt gun. To draw a bead on the ducks the punt itself was steered at them, while a skilled fowler could adjust the elevation of the gun by moving forward to depress the muzzle or wriggling into the stern of the craft to raise it.

Ernie James has had thirteen punt guns through his hands

Stalking ducks on the flooded washes was a solitary business and often a cold one too, when the freezing floodwaters chilled fingers to the bone as the fowler worked cautiously up to his quarry. But what tense excitement there was in the stalk, what split-second timing was required to make a successful shot. And what exquisite beauty there was in being afloat in the pink of a winter's dawn, when the feathered reed-heads were crusted with hoar frost and the whooper swans sounded a wild symphony overhead.

Returning from a day's punt gunning

Ernie spent many an hour as a boy just watching the gunners in the depths of winter quietly stalking up to the mallard and wigeon. He learned how to use every scrap of cover, every tuft of reed and every thistle-head which stood above the floodwaters, and to use the light to his advantage.

'The way to kill birds is to come out of the sun at them. Some weeks you could just fall in the boat and kill any number of birds. Another week and you couldn't get up to them.

'I loved it when I could hear where the ducks were in the dark and I would lay for a quarter of an hour without seeing them. As soon as it got light enough to see, I'd lay into 'em. Sometimes when I was not quick enough and they spotted me coming at them, one old duck would go quack and the whole lot would be off.'

A terrible thing for a professional fowler whose living depended on putting birds in the bag. But then hunting always was a risk business.

'Grandfather said if you wanted to be a gunner, you'd want ten pounds and a pig in the pot, and I reckon he were just about right.'

Ernie's best gunning days were during and just after the last war. In those dark days of food shortages a fat duck or a plover was eagerly snapped up by the hard-pressed housewife.

'When I first started, in 1927, ducks were five bob a pair, with wigeon half price, and you'd get fourpence for a plover. We'd reckon on getting two or three hundred in a good week.

'In 1947, the last seven days before we got frozen out, I got seven hundred birds, what with ducks and plovers, and made £700. There's been a time when I've had a thousand birds hanging in the cottage ready for market, and I once shot two stone of shot in a week . . . I used to kill 'em, one time o' day.'

His decision whether or not to fire the punt gun was a hard commercial one. If birds were a pound a pair, he would be quite prepared to expend a charge on just two ducks. Strangely, though, geese were worth no more than mallard to the dealer, and though an easy shot at geese might be snapped up, Ernie would prefer a chance at a dozen mallard.

With so many birds coming off the fens, the marketing and distribution system needed to be quite sophisticated. It relied on the railways, which took ducks by the tens of thousand to London, where they were sold in Leadenhall market. Some of the gunners delivered the birds themselves to the station by bike or handcart, while others relied on local carriers for transport to centres such as Ely.

By no means were all of these birds shot with punt and gun, however. In the old days there were the quiet, secluded decoy ponds with curved and tapering dykes leading off them. Wildfowl which settled on the pond were lured into the dykes by the decoyman and his dog, then driven into nets and killed. A decoy pond was a ruthlessly efficient killing engine which could provide a considerable profit to any estate which bordered onto the marshes, and many hundreds of them were built. Often they are still remembered today, perhaps in the name of a covert such as 'Decoy Wood', or maybe as a lonely flight pond. Much of my wildfowling on the Essex coast takes place just over the sea wall from such a pond, and the birds still whiffle into it at dusk in their dozens – a testimony to the skill with which the old timers sited their deadly duck traps. These days, however, that particular decoy pond is a sanctuary area, used by a wildfowling club as a release point for the hand-reared mallard with which they restock the marshes.

Ernie James was not a decoyman, but when there was no water on the washes, or when they were frozen over and it became impossible to use a punt, then he did have another way of taking wildfowl: by means of a 'battery'. When there was a big tide running in the Hundred Foot River, a likely looking patch of wash would be carefully flooded by allowing water through a series of channels or 'grips', and grain or frosted potatoes would be put down to encourage the ducks to use the tempting-looking piece of water. And when the wildfowl had grown accustomed to finding a ready meal there, the fowler would build himself a hide and would lay a punt gun or some similar large bore fowling piece in such a position as to cast a withering fire across the flooded wash.

With all prepared and the gun loaded and primed, he would return at night, crawling on his hands and knees, careful not to alarm any birds which might be feeding. Then it was a matter of waiting behind the screen of reeds until there were sufficient ducks within the killing zone, and letting drive with the big gun. Maybe he would pick up half a dozen, maybe twenty or more. Then the gun could be reloaded, and the fowler could wait for more ducks to arrive.

The battery was equally effective in snow and ice, when the washes were frozen over and punt gunning became impossible. In these conditions it was a case of cutting a hole in the ice and filling it with corn – the birds would pile in eagerly to mop up the free meal, scarcely suspecting what lay in store for them. To ensure that he remained invisible against the wintry background the gunner would wear a set of white overalls.

Until it was protected in 1954, the lapwing or green plover was killed in large quantities for the table, and the Welney washes were one of the centres for the art of plover netting, a skill in which Ernie James was a leading exponent. Plovers were caught in giant clap nets, powered by a spring which was released by means of a line that ran to the hide in which the fowler sat.

Preparing the ground for plover netting was an art in itself. First a raised rectangle of wash would be marked out, about forty yards long by twenty wide, in the centre of which the nets were to be set. Then the decoys were made ready. These were plovers which had been taken on some previous occasion, and which had been stuffed and dried.

With a stand of decoys in position, it was then up to the fowler to settle down into his hide and call in any passing birds with a shrill whistle. The plovers tumbled out of the sky, their reedy call sounding across the washes, and when there was a reasonable number in the centre of the nets, the cord was pulled and the trap sprung.

There seems little doubt that the netters made significant inroads into the plover population, though nothing in comparison to the terrible depletion which was subsequently caused by the draining of so many of our lowland wet meadows where the plovers used to breed. 'There haven't been the plovers here for years, like we used to know,' says Ernie sadly. Nevertheless, I must say that in the past two or three seasons I have been aware of increasing numbers of lapwings, grouped in huge flocks as they flight in from the fen farms at sunset, rising and spreading like a wraith of smoke in the far distance before settling onto the plashy pastures to feed.

As to the wigeon, however, Ernie maintains that there are just as many as there always were. 'The wigeon stay here now, some of them stay all summer, where in the old days they would all be gone by March. They've always been here on the washes, have the wigeon. 'Cept in the old days people didn't see them, only us that was in the washes all our lives.'

He looks at the washes today, sees the changes which have taken place over the last twenty years and shakes his head sadly.

'This gang has messed the washes up,' he says, pointing to the new bird reserves. 'They come down here with their red and yellow coats on, look in all the nests and frighten all the birds. The grass is so high you can't see a bullock in it: the birds, they need a clear place to land in. There's no place now for the waders, the washes want to be grazed right down.'

Neither do reserve managers have the same skill in controlling the floodwater as the old marsh shepherds. 'They don't know about making up the dams like we used to. They should have an L plate on 'em. I reckon these bird people are trying to mess all the washes up so they can buy them all up cheap. I think there's getting to be too many reserves. They want it all for themselves.'

But he has a scathing word or two to say about the wildfowlers as well. 'Today they're shooting at birds three gunshots high. They don't kill one in a dozen.' A far cry from the days when every shot had to be made to tell, and missed birds meant empty bellies.

Of course there were disappointments even in the old days, and especially when the big gun misfired, as it often did when water trickled down into the flash pan and dampened the priming powder. 'There was one time I couldn't have helped but kill forty. I got right up to 'em and the old gun misfired. Even then, they sat so tight that they let me get another cap out o' me weskit pocket. But they got up in the end and I never did get a shot.'

Ernie James was the last of the punt gunners on the washes at Welney. He kept on until the early 1970s with 'just a shot now and then'. But though retired from punt gunning he is far from inactive. They breed them tough in the fens: Ernie's mother lived to 108, and she was a sprightly old thing even then. There are still eels to catch and eel hives to weave on long winter nights, though more of them are sold these days as ornaments or curios to be turned into table lamps than ever are sunk with a length of chain into the river to soak, and then baited on a spring evening with fat, juicy lobworms.

As for shooting, it is hard to imagine Ernie ever losing his interest in the sport. He was born a wildfowler, and no doubt a wildfowler he will die. Even now he still gets out once or twice a season to bowl over a wild fen pheasant or to take a peek at the washes when the winter floods are up. And he is always ready for a gossip with the gunners when they return from evening flight, his eyes lighting up as out come the stories of the days when he shot the washes for a living. Yellowed photographs and careful records in meticulously maintained diaries are proffered in evidence.

But you know that when he is gone another link will be forever broken with a way of life that is now departed, an ancient and self-sufficient rural economy which the twentieth century has overwhelmed.

BROODIES AND GREEN TWEED

Keepering runs deep in George Oliver's blood. Son of a Herefordshire keeper, George left home at the age of fourteen to work as a gamekeeper's boy. With his seventieth birthday now behind him, he has clocked up fifty-seven years in the profession.

George Oliver receiving his long service medal from HM The Queen at the 1989 Game Fair

A longside the squire, the yeoman farmer, the village blacksmith, the parson and the poacher, the gamekeeper stands as one of the central characters of rural mythology. Clad in his heavy tweeds, gun under his arm and dog at heel, he strides the fields and woodlands of every popular picture of the countryside. Invariably he is typecast – sometimes as a Tom Forrest, amiable, avuncular and countrywise; elsewhere as the squire's own private policeman, stern and solitary, the man who boxes the ears of youthful apple scrumpers.

But as ever, the myth is an oversimplified version of reality. Today's gamekeeper is a skilled technician. His tools are the four-wheel-drive pickup, the CB radio, the automatic incubator and the infra-red intruder alarm. He is often responsible for managing an enormous annual budget, and the pressures upon him to show a successful return to his employer are as great as they are on any farm manager. The hours are long, the pay modest and the house often lonely and isolated. Yet amongst the gamekeeping profession one still finds a majority who, despite its disadvantages, have an abiding love for a job which keeps them out of doors, often as virtually their own bosses, working in a patch of country where they know each hedge, tree, fence and furrow. And, the acid test, gamekeepers are still proud when their sons follow in their footsteps.

Keepering runs deep in George Oliver's blood. Son of a north Herefordshire gamekeeper, George left home at the age of fourteen to work on the Gower Peninsula in south Wales as a gamekeeper's boy on the Clyne Castle estate of Admiral Walker-Heneage-Vivian, and with his seventieth birthday now behind him, he has clocked up fifty-seven years of continuous employment in the keepering profession, broken only by army service during the last war.

George Oliver (*left*) at Wrest Park. George is proud of the way he has turned the estate into a well-managed shoot

'I have always been with the keepers, ever since I was a boy. I either wanted to be a soldier or a keeper, and I've been both,' says George.

Gamekeeping in the thirties was a hard life, and when he was promoted to the post of beat keeper on the admiral's Parc le Breos estate at the age of seventeen, George was expected to work all hours on the rearing field whilst fetching and carrying for just about everyone in the game department as well.

'When I arrived on the estate, them old keepers looked me up and down and said "Right young George, here's the list". Then they gave me a list and three damn great stone jars. When I asked them what the jars were for, I was told that they were for the beer. And it was my job to walk the four miles there and back to the pub at Barland every day to fetch the keepers' baccy and their beer. I used to take the shortest route up and down three steep combes, carrying these three stone jars, without any barrow or anything like that, but it still used to be half past eleven when I got back onto the rearing field. And by heavens, when I got back I knew that I had done some work.'

There was plenty of fetching and carrying to be done in those days, for such things as Land-Rovers were unheard of. A keeper was expected to walk his beat, and at feeding time he carried his bulging bag of pheasant food on his shoulder. It was the same when it came to collecting the broody hens that were used to hatch the pheasant eggs before the days of incubators. They, too, had to be fetched from the local farmyards. As a young keeper, George would have to call on the farmers to ask if they had any broodies and then search the barns and haysheds to find them, bringing his haul of thumping great Light Sussex or Rhode Island Reds back to the rearing coops, five to a sack. And woe betide him if the head keeper found anything wrong with any one of them, some disorder which might conceivably be transmitted to the pheasant chicks, for then George would have to take the whole lot straight back to the farms again.

The game rearing season marks the start of the keeper's year, and today it often centres around a visit to the game farm where pheasants or partridges can be purchased as day-olds or poults. That was not the way on the traditional estate, where all the eggs were produced from hen pheasants caught up by the keeper at the end of the shooting season. George still catches up his hens with the aid of a special bait, the recipe of which is a closely guarded secret.

'In those days the hen pheasants didn't produce as many eggs as they do now. At the outside we only used to get twenty-five or twenty-six eggs per hen. We used to put the hens in a big open-topped pen, about four acres in size, one cock to six hens, and it used to take us three hours to pick up all the eggs. You'd have to search all in the spinneys and the bushes for them.'

Once the eggs were gathered, they were put under broodies in coops arranged in rows out on the rearing field. The hens were tethered by one leg to a hazel stick, so that when the keeper took them off the nest for ten minutes to feed them he could be sure of putting the right hen back on each clutch of eggs. The old keepers believed that the body temperature varied with different hens, and that changing the broodies would affect the hatching rate.

'Before you put the hens back, you had to clean all the droppings off with a shovel and a scraper. That went in a heap and used to go on the head keeper's garden. In my spare time I had to dig it in', George recalls.

It was a highly labour intensive business, and it was no wonder that estates ran large game departments in those days. On the admiral's two estates at Clyne Castle and Parc le Breos there was a total of nine gamekeepers, plus three woodmen, who were also attached to the game department.

Even when the young birds were hatched there was no let-up:

'In those days there were always two keepers sitting out with the pheasants, looking after them and shutting them up at night. When you got a muggy night, the darned things would sit around the back of the coop instead of going in under the broody hens, and sometimes you'd be on the field shutting up until eleven or twelve o'clock at night.

'Then two keepers used to be up at half past four in the morning for the first feed at five o'clock. We fed at five o'clock, half past eleven, half past three and half past six at night.'

LEFT
The gamekeeper – a central character in rural mythology

Preparing the food was just as time-consuming as feeding it to the birds. All today's keeper has to do is to telephone the game feed merchant and his order will arrive promptly in twenty-five kilo sacks, specially formulated to exacting nutritional standards. A far cry from prewar days when George and his colleagues would have to scald great quantities of maize in a boiler and then mix in thousands of eggs imported from Poland in crates. The boiled mixture was pressed through a fine sieve before biscuit meal and meat was added.

George stopped rearing pheasants under broodies twenty years ago. At the time he was working as gamekeeper to Sir Francis Appleyard at Stevenage, Hertfordshire, a post he held for twenty-two years, from when he came out of the army in 1950 until the death of his employer and the break-up of the estate. He brought all his rearing equipment with him to Wrest Park, at Silsoe in Bedfordshire, where since 1972 he has been keeper to Mr Tony Burton over the two thousand acre Home Farm.

Game shooting has become increasingly popular in recent years

'When I moved here there was nothing except vermin. Plenty of weasels, stoats and foxes. Everything except game. I found one pheasant's nest on two thousand acres, and we used to go down the concrete roads on the estate and say "Oh look, a pheasant!" There was a part-time keeper then, and he used to put down twelve hundred pheasants, bought in as day olds, and they would shoot three hundred in a season if they were lucky.'

George is proud of the way in which he has turned the estate into a well managed shoot, largely by careful attention to game rearing.

'I brought all my own incubators and my laying pens here with me. I hatch in still air incubators, seven of them. I don't go in for these mod-con things they have now. Night and morning I turn nineteen hundred eggs by hand, and last year I averaged out at eighty per cent success rate.'

He places a great deal of faith in his ancient, tried and trusted equipment, amongst which there is one old incubator which he bought off another keeper for twenty-five pounds.

'It's called a Mendip. Well, I'd never heard of a Mendip before, and I reckon that must be a hundred years old. It's fuelled by paraffin and all patched up with wire. I never saw anything like it in my life. When I got to pull out the chick tray for the first time, the bottom dropped out and all the chicks fell into the bottom of the incubator. But out of two hundred eggs, I took a hundred and fifty nine chicks out of that old incubator, and it will stop dead at 104°F no matter whether the weather's hot, cold or anything.'

Since the war George has always been a singlehanded keeper, and even on the big estates it is rare now to find the larger gamekeeping establishments which were once the norm. Traditionally the rule was that one gamekeeper would look after a thousand acres and rear a thousand pheasants. Now a singlehanded man is expected to do many times that amount. The Home Farm at Wrest Park is not large by the standards of some shoots which a single keeper must look after today, but it is big enough for a seventy year old, even one

as sprightly and agile as George Oliver. He is lucky in the topography of the estate. Formerly the property of the de Grey family, Wrest Park was laid out for shooting, with coverts, shelter belts and copses strategically placed to provide high, sporting pheasants off the rolling hills which surround the big house. Then it ran to around ten thousand acres. Although these days the house is part of the National Institute of Agricultural Engineering, once you are beyond the laboratories and engineering workshops the place still has very much the feel of an old estate about it, down to the de Grey family coat of arms carved in stone above the door of George's lodge cottage.

Nevertheless, the days when there was a vast staff of liveried servants are long gone. George remembers such times on the Gower Peninsula, when the pay was meagre and the hours were long.

'Before I went to Parc le Breos I was getting fourteen shillings a week. I was paying the head keeper's wife ten shillings a week for lodgings and so I had four bob to myself. Then the head keeper that I was with took over at Parc le Breos and I was offered a job as beat keeper. I shall always remember the old admiral sitting there, saying "He's been a very good boy since he's been with us. We'll give him a chance for twelve months". After that I got a four bob rise to eighteen shillings a week, and a damn good suit of clothes supplied.

'I had boxcloth leggings, a green trilby hat and a pair of boots made to measure by Pope and Jacksons in Swansea. They alone used to cost thirty-five shillings. You used to go and have your feet measured and then a fortnight later you had the boots fitted. After that they used to be delivered to the castle. They were made of horse hide and would last for two years. All the keepers wore the same green tweeds, and we all had the Vivian crest on our jackets and on the buttons of our waistcoats.

'The old keepers never had holidays in the middle of the rearing season. If you wanted a week's holiday, then you took it in February or March after the shooting was over and before you started rearing. And you only had a week. Some of those old keepers on the Gower Peninsula would maybe go to Swansea once or twice a year, and I've known old keepers that have never gone off the estate.'

It is a different story today, and George looks askance at some of the present generation of keepers, who by his rigorous standards are overpaid and underworked.

'There are some good keepers around today, and some damned bad ones, and I reckon that some of the bad ones have got the best jobs. I know one or two keepers, I've seen them while I've been working, and they're off playing golf at ten thirty in the morning. I've even heard of one going on a week's golfing tournament down at Brighton, and a fortnight afterwards he took his wife to Tenerife! This year I heard he'd been deerstalking in Scotland.'

George himself has taken three days off in the last three years, on one of which he was ill in bed.

Traditionally there has never been any formal training available to those who seek to enter the gamekeeping profession. In the old days you were born to the job and served your apprenticeship. But now all that is changing. The opportunities to work in countryside wardening and wildlife management as well as traditional keepering have increased, and in consequence a number of practical courses have evolved, most of them based at the agricultural colleges, at which keepering skills can be acquired in the context of a formal and structured programme of education. That is not to say that all those who

High birds over the guns on a frosty morning

gain their qualification with the aim of a career in gamekeeping manage to find jobs. It is reckoned that there are only around five thousand full time gamekeepers in Britain today, a substantial decline from the position of thirty years ago, and jobs for new entrants to the profession are keenly sought after.

It may well be that the enormous growth in the popularity of game shooting which has been witnessed in the 1980s has created more jobs in gamekeeping and served at least to halt the decline, if not reverse it. But there is still keen competition when a trainee keeper's job comes up. The Youth Training Scheme is a regular starting point for a career on the keepering ladder, and while some boys go on to make the grade, others do not have what it takes to satisfy an experienced man like George Oliver.

He was once offered a boy by his employer, a well recommended lad who, it was hoped, would be able to help out on the rearing field. The boy was not much of a hit with George. Things got off to a bad start when, in the course of being taught how to set a trap, he cut his finger with a penknife and took half of the following day off to go to the doctor. To a former battery sergeant major who had fought his way across France, North Africa and Italy, that did not exactly strike the right chord. Nor did the boy's marksmanship.

'I gave him two hundred and fifty cartridges and a twelve bore shotgun, and off he went every day, disappearing until dinner time. I had no idea where he was, and I wasn't going to start looking around for him. About a fortnight afterwards he said to me "Can I use your sixteen bore?" Now I always shoot with a sixteen bore and I don't like anyone else using it, so I said to him "What's the matter? You've got a twelve bore and plenty of cartridges". So he told me that he'd only got five cartridges left. In two weeks he'd got through two hundred and fifty cartridges and all he brought back in that time was one rook and a flipping pigeon for the ferret.

'Then one day he brought a stoat back and I could see it had been shot. So I told him he'd done a jolly good job and asked where he'd shot it. He told me it was in one of my traps under a tree stump. He'd shot the flipping stoat in the trap and blown the trap to smithereens.

'Another time he told me he was going off to get some magpies, and I asked him how he was going to do that. He said that he was going to hide in the woods with a box of matches, then he'd shake the matches and all the magpies would come to him. So I sent him down to the woods and he came back at four o'clock. "Where's the magpies, then?" I asked him, and he said they never came. He told me that was some bright idea he'd read in the *Shooting Times*. He was a daft lad, was that one.'

Wrest Park is what George describes as a farmers' shoot. Indeed, many of the guests are members of the local farming community, but a fair sprinkling of the mighty names of the agricultural world have shot there, presidents of the National Farmers Union and Ministers of Agriculture alike. In the early days things were not quite so grand, and it was quite a change for George when he arrived there after having worked on Sir Francis Appleyard's estate.

'When I first came here I saw all these fellows standing about looking like scarecrows, and I said to one of the old beaters who always used to come and beat here "Who on earth are these? They aren't the blokes I asked to come and beat" and he said "No, they're not the beaters, they're the Guns!"'

'Well, all these fellows were dressed in old jackets and overalls. They were all the old farmers, and I hadn't been used to that sort of thing. But I tell you one thing, they've changed over the last seventeen years, and now they wear some of the finest shooting suits I've ever seen.'

But although the familiar guests are known and trusted, a difficult moment always comes for the keeper when he discovers that one of the Guns is inexperienced or even downright dangerous. It requires a nice judgement to decide how to handle the matter with least embarrassment to his employer and at least risk of bodily harm to himself and his beaters.

One visiting Gun whom George had to deal with when he worked at Stevenage was a foreigner of teutonic extraction. It became obvious that things were going to be a little fraught when George noticed that the barrels of his drilling – a three-barrelled weapon, popular in Germany, in which the two side-by-side shotgun barrels have a rifled barrel mounted beneath them – were stuffed with cotton wool. One of the most elementary lessons of gun safety is that any obstruction in a shotgun, however insignificant, is capable of bursting the barrels and seriously injuring the shooter. So the guest was approached with extreme tact.

Shortly afterwards, the Guns lined out at the far end of a strip of kale which was being brought down by the beaters. As the drive neared its conclusion, out came a cock pheasant, low over the Guns, at which the foreign guest upped with his piece and let drive, peppering six or seven of the beaters in the process. George had seen quite enough. He pulled the beaters out and stopped the drive. When Sir Francis hurried up and asked what the matter was, George's remarks were short and to the point.

'You can tell that fellow not to shoot me. I'm not going to stand here and be shot by him, I've been shot at by those b***s quite enough in the past!'

Eventually the beaters were prevailed upon to continue with the shoot, but a 'loader' was detailed to stand with the visitor for the rest of the day. A week later a crate of port arrived for the benefit of George and his friends, but even though honour was satisfied, the foreigner was never invited to shoot there again.

Another possible area of embarrassment surrounds the practice of tipping. Gamekeepers on the whole are not well paid, and rely to a substantial extent on the tips which they receive from the visiting guns throughout the course of the season. There is an unwritten code of practice where tipping is concerned, and on the larger, more opulent shoots, tips can be quite substantial; yet there are always a few Guns who fail to discharge their gentlemanly duties with an appropriate degree of generosity.

On one estate where George used to go picking up, the Guns used to give the keepers their cartridge bags to carry on the less formal 'outside days', following which they would normally offer a tip of half a crown. After one shoot a certain old gentleman came up and approached the keeper who had been helping him throughout the course of the day, and, thanking him, pressed three coins into the keeper's hand. Naturally, the keeper's spirits leaped at the thought of possible riches, and he quickly withdrew to a discreet distance at which he could examine the spoils. It turned out to be threepence.

Nothing daunted, he called out 'Excuse me, sir!' 'Yes, keeper, what's the matter?' replied the Gun. 'I should think you'll need this to go home on the bus,' quipped the young keeper tartly, offering up the copper pennies.

Alas, those were strict, hard times. The Gun told the shoot owner, who in turn told his agent and the keeper was dismissed on the spot.

When carried out correctly, however, tipping in the shooting field is an art form. The offering is folded in the palm of the Gun's right hand and transferred to the keeper with utmost discretion. It is a time-honoured tradition, and one which most keepers, at least those of the older generation, prefer. George hates the way in which some Guns today peel off two ten pound notes from a wad which they carry in their pocket, and flourish them at him for all the world to see.

'I don't like that. When I used to go shooting with the admiral, he would go quietly up to the head keeper and shake him by the hand saying "There you are, keeper, thank you for a lovely day" and the keeper would never know what he'd got until afterwards.'

The gamekeeper's traditional adversary is the poacher, a character who has as much, if not more mythology spun around him than the keeper himself. The popular image of the poacher is that of a likeable village rogue with a nondescript lurcher, who slips a rabbit, hare or pheasant into his back pocket on a moonlit night. He is almost a class hero, a man who is prepared to put one over on the gentry at the risk of cruel punishment if he is caught. But the days of transportation to the colonies are over and the setting of man traps in the coverts, vicious engines of terror which would take a poacher's leg off, went out with public hanging.

Poaching today is big business, especially the taking of deer and salmon. In Wales it is now reckoned that more salmon are landed illegally each year than are caught by licensed sportsmen and netsmen, and on the Scottish Tweed, where the River Commissioners distribute the fish which they confiscate from poachers to the local old peoples' homes, it is said that elderly folk are getting fed up with eating salmon. Deer poaching is also a serious problem, and one which causes enormous suffering. For whereas the legitimate stalker employs a fullbore rifle to take his deer, the poacher depends upon snares and lurchers to either strangle the deer, trap them by the leg or pull them down, normally against a woodland fence. Sometimes crossbows or shotguns are used, weapons which are quite unsuitable for shooting deer at normal sporting range, and which generally result in pitifully wounded animals left to die a lingering death.

Much of today's poaching is related to the motor car. Years ago, poachers were generally local people whom the gamekeeper knew, and even if he did not condone their activities, then at least, provided they remained on a small scale, they did not cause him too much trouble. Nowadays the small-scale poacher will work with an air rifle out of a car window, while the poaching gangs plan their operations with precision – they will clean out a wood in an hour or so at night and be a hundred miles away by daybreak.

RIGHT
The picker-up with his dogs – vital members of the team on a shooting day

Where poaching is a serious problem, keepers now endure threats to their property, their families and even their lives. The dog which walks at a gamekeeper's heel is now as likely to be an alsatian as a labrador, and the keeper or his employer might spend vast sums of money on radio-linked tripwire alarms or infra-red detection equipment. It is a far cry from the Arcadian myth. However, these days George Oliver has few real problems with poaching. Admittedly he keeps a wary eye open for the lurcher men who stray onto the estate to take hares and rabbits, and is always suspicious of any strange car which he sees tucked into some roadside verge, but large-scale night poaching does not worry him.

In the past, on the Gower Peninsula, it was a different matter. George has been beaten up and even knifed by poachers. On that occasion an offender had been raiding the woods for several days and the keepers were determined to catch him, taking it in turns to lie in wait. One morning George spotted the man and challenged him. Although only seventeen at the time, he went for the poacher, who drew a knife and lunged at him, the blade going clean through George's hand. Nothing daunted, he hit the fellow over the head and took him to the head keeper, who summoned the police. The poacher was duly prosecuted.

Sometimes the poachers came in gangs of up to ten, and there were set-piece battles between them and the keepers. Once a gang of eight poachers was spotted on a sunken lane with high banks and a barbed wire fence. The police had been called and every available member of the estate staff was roused, but the poachers decided to make a break for it, climbed the bank, scaled the fence and ran across a field. Then, realising that they were surrounded, they turned and fought, first pelting the keepers with stones, then using their fists. One strapping big fellow only had one arm, so, thinking that he would be an easy arrest, the head keeper went for him. But he proved more than a match for the keeper, getting his one good arm around him, lifting him clean off the ground and shaking him like a terrier shakes a rat. George stood there and laughed. The one-armed bandit turned out to be a regular customer, and he was soon dubbed 'Wingy'.

'He'd never tackle me, old Wingy. If I caught him, he'd say "Oh well, it's a fair catch" and he used to go quietly with me to the police. I would give evidence against him in court, then wait outside and when he came out I'd say "Come on, we'll have a drink now." But he'd always try to have it back off me within a few days.'

Wingy was probably closer than most to the traditional picture of the poacher, and sometimes he even managed to wrong-foot the keepers. Once George caught him on the estate, looking as though he was up to no good. His shirt was bulging and it was obvious that contraband was hidden within. But when he lifted it up, it contained not pheasants but a couple of Rhode Island Reds and a load of cooking apples!'

With more than his threescore years and ten behind him, George will not even contemplate retirement. His fierce loyalty and his long service have already won him public recognition in the form of the coveted gamekeepers' long service medal, presented at the Country Landowners Association Game Fair at Stratfield Saye by Her Majesty The Queen. It was a great honour, but the big public occasion is not something which George normally relishes. Like many older gamekeepers, he is content with his own company. He has no time for radio or television, and prefers to be by his own cottage fireside with a good book.

But above all, George Oliver is at his happiest when out in the woods with only the wild creatures and his pheasants around him.

UNDER THE MOON

Moonflighting is the most exciting, most romantic form of shoulder gunning around the coasts. Often lonely, often cold, sometimes with the spice of danger and always hard work, it has drawn generations of wildfowlers to the marsh at night.

Wildfowling – lonely, cold and with the
spice of danger

The December full moon coincided with what looked to be perfect conditions for wildfowling on the east coast: a post-Christmas cold snap and a northerly wind with the promise of snow which would be guaranteed to bring the migratory wildfowl down onto the estuary. As I looked out of the window at the rising moon, the feathery banks of high cirrus clouds were already showing in the west, and with a midnight tide predicted, there was every prospect of a shot or two at the wigeon as they moved off their feeding grounds to flight into the flooded saltings just before high water.

It was an opportunity I just had to take. There are few enough nights each season upon which weather conditions and the state of the tide combine with the moon's phases to make possible a trip below the sea wall after dark, and a chance like this was not to be missed. In theory it might be bright enough in the moonlight to shoot perhaps three nights on either side of each full moon from September through to January or February, but theory takes no account of the weather, and in particular the cloud cover upon which the wildfowler depends in order to be able to see his quarry.

Moonflighting is only feasible when the sky is covered with high or medium level cloud, a veil of cirrostratus perhaps, through which the moon gleams milky white and is bedecked with a glistening halo. Or even better, a mackerel sky replete with pearly banks of altocumulus. For it is the cloud cover which forms the necessary backdrop against which to shoot. Too much cloud and the fowler is plunged into murky, muddy gloom, unable even to pick his way in safety across the foreshore. Too little and any birds which might be on the move will become totally invisible. Against the starry blackness of a cloudless night sky, any amount of wildfowl can fly unseen, unless they should for a split second pass tantalisingly across the moon's silver disc.

After an early supper I got my fowling gear together – Barbour, waders, cut-off waterproof leggings to keep me dry as the salt marsh flooded at high water, game bag with Thermos flask, wading stick, cartridges and gun. For night shooting it is best to use something handy like a lightweight twelve with game borings, as the birds almost always appear out of nowhere at close range and you generally have only a split second to get onto them before they disappear into the gloom. Some wildfowlers swear by a twenty bore at night, and there is no doubt that a lively and pointable twenty in the right pair of hands is a highly effective gun for moonflighting. The heavy double ten, my regular foreshore gun, remained at home in the gun cabinet and my light, twelve bore game gun was selected in its stead.

One last look at the sky confirmed that conditions were good. If anything they were getting better by the minute. Banks of fleecy altocumulus raced across the moon as I walked down the path to Teal's kennel, slipped the latch and led her, bouncing and skipping with excitement, towards the car.

It was a twenty-five minute drive to the marsh, and, turning off the main road, we bumped down the long, gravelled farm track in plenty of time, passing the farmhouse with its warm lights peeking from behind drawn living-room curtains as we did so. It was slightly odd to think that inside they were just about to settle down for the evening in front of the fire and watch the nine o'clock news, whereas Teal and I would be spending the next three hours or so exposed on a wet and freezing salt marsh, keeping our appointment with birds which had travelled hundreds, maybe thousands of miles from northern Scandinavia or arctic Russia to be here on this same cold, windswept, moonlit night.

I parked in the darkened farm yard, struggled into my waders and quickly zipped up my heavy waxed fowling coat against the cold which stung, keen and cutting after the warmth of the car. Then together, Teal and I walked down the long chase which leads from the farm to the sea wall, crunching our way towards the distant tideline across grass laced with hoar frost and through puddles frozen bone-hard in the bitter cold of a midwinter's night. Over my left shoulder the wind played tunes down the barrels of my gun, moaning flute-like as it blew diagonally across the muzzles. It was freshening to about force four, or so it felt, and had swung round perceptibly a few points into the east. But still the cloud cover looked good, and there was plenty more altocumulus massing to windward on the horizon. The temperature was plummeting, and I was glad to have brought a pair of full-fingered woollen mittens with me to maintain at least some semblance of circulation in my fingertips. Labradors don't seem to care about such minor irritants as cold, however, and Teal was wantonly crashing through the ice into the freezing waters of a flooded dyke, then rolling and cavorting on the frosted grass like a puppy.

Soon we were passing the old reclaimed saltings. Now embanked and drained, the contours of the former creeks stood out from the rabbit-cropped grass and the frozen splashes of rainwater in the maze of shallow depressions showed unmistakable signs of where ducks had been grazing before the frost – telltale white breast feathers and scattered droppings lay amongst the coarse sedges. Then beyond, just a hundred yards further down the chase, loomed the dark bulk of the sea wall.

A short climb and a few steps later and we had crossed into another world. At any time the salt marsh is a special place, but under the pale, ghostly light of the full moon it is magical. Over the chill whiteness of ice-glazed grass and the ragged, decayed remains of sea lavender and sea aster, from the tumble of winding creeks, their sticky wet beds bright in the moonlight, comes the tang of salt, the piping of oystercatcher and redshank and, as ears are strained, the hoarse quacking of a distant mallard moving up on the tideline.

We were quite alone. Wildfowling on the whole tends to be a solitary sport, but in daylight hours there is always the feeling that someone, somewhere, has his eyes open to whatever is happening on the estuary, whether it be a bait digger, fisherman, birdwatcher or simply a passing dog walker. At night, though, there is just the vast bowl of the

heavens, surrounded by the twinkling lights of a few isolated farmsteads and, away to the south, a glow from the distant villages beyond the broad, dark wastes of the river. It's cold; there are just the moon, stars and dog for company, but it's intensely exciting and all of a sudden there's a sense of adventure in the air.

I caught the chill of the breeze against my face as I turned on the top of the sea wall to climb the stile and make my way along to where the main tidal gutter cuts the marsh in two. With around three hours to go before high water, the first fingers of the making tide were already feeling their way across its muddy bed, little flecks of scum around their edges. It is fifty yards wide at this point, and although quite safe to cross at low water, the gutter floods rapidly, cutting off one line of retreat to safety. That is something which every coastal wildfowler has at the back of his mind – the overriding thought of personal survival. What one minute is an innocent-looking creek, readily fordable in a pair of waders, may half an hour later become a wide and angry stretch of water, grey, foam-flecked and racing with a strong tidal current that bars your access to the security of the sea wall. It is bad enough to get trapped in such a situation during daylight hours, when you may be lucky and get away with a soaking and a bad fright, but at night on a big flood tide, with only the moon to hear your cries for help, it is a different and far more deadly matter. No wildfowler ever gets caught out by the tide more than once if he can help it. It is just that, for the unlucky few, there is no second chance.

Once across the gutter, I climbed up onto the saltings proper, and made my way along a shingle spit lined with sueda bushes. Moving quietly, cautiously, looking and listening for any sign or sound of wildfowl movement, I headed for the last little knot of shrubby growth which stands guard over the marsh.

As I rested for a few minutes in the bushy cover, there was a movement to my left and out of the moon came four mallard, low, straight and on course to pass directly overhead. At least one of them, maybe even two should have been safely in the bag, but I mounted the gun in haste and swung onto the leader ineptly, punching a hole into the inky blackness a good three feet behind him, too astonished at my own incompetence even to fire a second barrel. The wildfowler can expect few chances as good as that in an outing, and to miss so comprehensively is intensely frustrating. I cursed my stupidity.

Though the breeze quickly whipped away the sound of my shot, a pair of curlews shrieked their protest, an indignant chorus of alarm calls echoing across the foreshore muds as the brent geese set up a nervous chatter. But the spring tide had yet two and a half hours to run, and there was still plenty of cover in the big creeks on the front of the marsh, so Teal and I moved down to flight the tide.

Tide flighting tends to be the best means of making the most of a night's shooting under the moon. At dawn and dusk, wildfowl movement is concentrated into a relatively brief period of the day, during which the shooter can do his best to get beneath whatever flight line he may see developing, or simply to settle down in some favoured location. On a shiny night, however, ducks are likely to be on the move at any time between the rising and setting of the moon, unless some other factor comes into the equation. On the foreshore, the twice daily ebb and flow of the tide exerts a powerful influence over the birds of the estuary, just as it does over every other living occupant, be it plant or animal.

At low water the fowl feed far out on the intertidal muds, but as the flooding tide gradually covers their feeding grounds, they are forced off the foreshore, first congregating about the tide's edge, then moving in little groups and larger packs up onto the higher saltings where they can ride out the high tide in some flooded creek, or perhaps feed on the seeds that are left clinging to the dead marsh grasses or washed up amongst the debris and jetsam along the high water mark. Thus the bulk of tide-influenced wildfowl movement is concentrated into the three hours before high water, and it is therefore at this period that the shooter is likely to achieve most success.

A reasonable wind is also important to the chances of the night-time fowler, as it keeps the birds on the move and forces them to seek the shelter of creek or salting. A still night, though it might be a beautiful one on which to sit out on the marsh, is likely to see the ducks roosting on the main channel of the estuary, where they can float on the calm water in peace until the feeding grounds are once again exposed. All that will be heard on such a night is the frustrating sound of quackings and whistlings coming from the wide waters.

As I waited and watched from my chosen creek, the saltings came to life. All about me were the sounds of wildfowl, an object lesson to anyone who might consider that the problem of positive quarry recognition makes moonflighting a practical impossibility. Quite apart from the notes of the birds themselves – the whistle of wigeon and peep of teal as they move through the gloom, or the laughter of shelduck and cronk of brent on the tideline – the sound of the wingbeat of each species is quite distinctive. Teal close at hand make a rushing noise like the tearing of newspaper; wigeon and mallard both send the wind whistling through their pinions, the mallard's wingbeat being the more rhythmical of the two. The beats of the shelduck and brent are much slower altogether, and no experienced fowler is likely to mistake them for those of one of the quarry ducks. The sound of wing and voice gives that vital split second's warning of a potential shot presenting itself and this, when combined with the picture of the ducks themselves, silhouetted against the clouds, makes for surprisingly accurate identification. Nevertheless, the wildfowler must still be a competent ornithologist as well as a good shot if he is to make the most of the time he spends on the marsh.

More perceptive even than human senses are those of the wildfowler's dog, and as Teal stiffened her neck and cocked her ears into the night sky, I swung round to see two mallard sweep low over the marsh behind me. In a fraction of a second I was onto the right-hand bird and, firing the cylinder barrel, I watched it dip out of sight below the blackness of the horizon as its partner flared away into the dark. Teal had marked the direction in which the bird had dropped and was instantly off about her business while I waited and hoped. I could only guess at the chase she had across the rapidly flooding mudflats, though I followed her progress by reference to the splashes as she galloped through the water and the sticky plowtering of pads in mud as she headed back across an empty creek. When, what seemed like hours later, she reappeared carrying a plump mallard in her soft mouth, there was no better dog in England. Or, for that matter, a happier wildfowler. Without her that would have been a lost bird – but there again, without her I would have had no business being out on the marsh by night at all.

By now the banks of cloud were racing across the moon, which seemed to dodge between them, bathing the marsh in brilliant light and turning the river to liquid silver as it scurried across the intervening velvet blackness of the night. Cloud shadows chased each other over the marsh and a scattering of stars appeared in each cloud gap, to be snuffed quickly as the next pearl-grey slab made its hurried advance. A cock pheasant crowed on the distant uplands, setting off its fellows for miles around. For a full minute the crowing lasted, echoing across the estuary as a labrador's ears quivered with excitement.

RIGHT
The tang of salt and piping waders – sunset over an Essex creek

Like so many facets of wildfowling, moonflighting is practised by only a small minority of shooters. Thus over the years it has regularly found itself under the scrutiny of legislators both here in Britain and overseas on the European mainland, and sniped at by those who want to see the traditions which make wildfowling in Britain so unique whittled away in the grey cause of international uniformity.

Wildfowlers have been at pains to maintain the integrity of night shooting and it is essential that they continue to do so. There are many areas around the coast where it would be quite possible to shoot at night throughout the season under industrial lights, irrespective of the phases of the moon. Yet in every case where this possibility arises, self-regulation, mostly by the wildfowling clubs which control the sporting rights over most of the shootable foreshore in England and Wales, has ensured that unfair advantage is not taken over the birds. Night shooting is invariably confined, for those who seek it, to a couple of days on either side of the full moon.

Among the criticisms which have been levelled at night shooting is that it might cause undue disturbance to wildfowl which are endeavouring either to roost or feed. Disturbance is a thorny question amongst wildfowlers and conservationists alike, for no shooter wilfully sets about disturbing ducks. Indeed, he does his utmost to remain hidden on the marsh, using hides and camouflaged clothing to help him do so. I have regularly had waders feeding around the edge of my hide whilst I have been tide flighting, quite oblivious to my presence. There is no doubt that the sound of shooting causes some disturbance, as does walking across the saltings in order to get to and from the flighting position. But the disturbance is not great when put alongside other activities on today's estuaries – sailing, windsurfing, bait digging, water skiing, recreational walking along the sea wall and the movement of aircraft of all sorts, from hang gliders and helicopters to military jet fighters.

In the past, particularly in the days before and shortly after the last war when the grey geese were relentlessly shot on their roosts at night, the disturbance caused by moonflighting was certainly a serious problem. Indeed, it contributed to some noted goose roosts being entirely abandoned for decades. Today, thanks again in no small measure to the controls exercised by the wildfowling clubs, disturbance of roosting geese is no longer a problem and in general the growing network of refuges ensures that wildfowl of all sorts have sufficient sanctuary areas at their disposal.

Moonflighting is reckoned by many to be the cream of wildfowling. Certainly it is the most exciting, most romantic form of shoulder gunning around the coasts. Often lonely, often cold, sometimes with the spice of danger and always hard work, it has drawn generations of wildfowlers to the marsh at night when, without that small spark of adventure, they would otherwise be sitting beside a warm fire or tucked up safely in bed.

On these things I mused as I made my way back to the car. It would probably be two in the morning before I finally got to bed, but I had chosen probably the best night of the winter on which to shoot under the moon. Now the stars were disappearing behind a thin veil and a halo was forming around the moon itself. It would not be long before the cloud thickened and the snow which had been promised would start to fall. I would be lucky to see any sort of moon at all on the following night, but snow would no doubt bring other compensations, other opportunities. To the keen wildfowler it always does.

A WARRENER'S BRECK

Straddling the borders of Norfolk and Suffolk, Elveden was a wild country which dropped from the sandy breckland down to a miry wilderness of black fen. Virtually useless as farm land, it was devoted to the partridge, the pheasant and the rabbit.

Scots pines, gnarled and blasted, straggle across the breckland skyline

Like malevolent monsters they lumber across the darkening tarmac, great grey shapes, sinister shadows behind the red runway lights, lurching and rumbling as they turn, one after another, towards the bloodshot west. Then a roar like the drums of doom, a deep, pounding snarl which sets the ground shuddering and spits forth blue tongues of flame. Catapulting forward, the monsters bound down the runway, screeching, bouncing, till with one final gargantuan effort they rise towards the evening's glow, two dense plumes of acrid black smoke tracking them into the gathering night. The roar drops to a distant rumble, then dies to a whisper. A brooding quiet returns to Lakenheath air base as the squat shape of the control tower stands silhouetted against the gloom.

It is a scene which is repeated day after day, night after night at this, the front line of NATO's air defence shield. From here and from a dozen bases like it the air forces of the Western powers manoeuvre, practise and probe. Lakenheath, Mildenhall, Marham, Coltishall, Sculthorpe, Bentwaters – names familiar to generations of airmen. Where today the Jaguar, F16, Tornado and A10 wield a menace backed by the awful power of the nuclear age, so too did the B17s, Lancasters and Spitfires set out to challenge the might of Nazi Germany. For thousands of young men from Nebraska and Northampton, Oxford and Oregon, those lonely East Anglian acres were the last they walked upon, that control tower and the clump of three gnarled and ancient greengage trees standing beside it their final marker before eternity.

For half a century the allied air forces have flown from Lakenheath, and it is only now, when East and West are being drawn together in a fragile new framework of democratic freedom, that there is the prospect of peaceful skies over breckland. For already there are whispers of what might be when NATO no longer needs to station its airmen here.

But there was a time before the Phantom or Flying Fortress. A time even before the Forestry Commission came to clothe these parts with their gloomy plantations of pine and spruce, a time when three greengage trees grew amidst a rambling cottage garden on the edge of Lakenheath warren. When a young lad carried nets, traps and ferrets for his father as he eagerly learned the craft of the warrener. In those days, before the outbreak of the Kaiser's war, that land was part of Lord Iveagh's Elveden estate. Straddling the borders of Norfolk and Suffolk, it was a wild country which dropped from the sandy heath and gorse of the breckland down to a miry wilderness of black fen. Virtually useless as far as arable farming was concerned, it was devoted to the partridge, the pheasant and the rabbit.

The countryside around Elveden itself had been laid out for sport. Under its previous and celebrated owner Prince Duleep Singh, it had become one of the greatest shooting estates in England, regularly playing host to the leading sportsmen of the Edwardian era. But there was also another side to the local economy, the humble bunny: countless tens of thousands of rabbits inhabited the heathland round about, and so numerous were they that not a tree or bush grew on Lakenheath warren. It ran for miles, flat acres of close-cropped turf and patches of bracken which even the rabbits would not stomach, interspersed with moving dunes of windblown sand. In fact the breckland sands were at one time so unstable that they resembled the dunes of a north African desert, sufficiently large to overwhelm a whole village, as happened in 1668 when the old village of Santon was buried in a sandstorm.

On a summer's evening the warren would be an undulating carpet of white cotton tails and twitching ears, an insuperable obstacle to the farmer and like to devour any blade of corn that had the impertinence to poke its head out of the ground. And in the fogs of winter the warren was a place to be dreaded – crossed only by the ancient Shaker's road, the benighted traveller could all too easily lose himself on its treeless plain.

Yet the rabbits themselves were a valuable commodity, the central feature of a thriving local trade, and in time the warren was surrounded with a series of great earthen banks, four and a half feet high, perpendicular on their inner sides and sloping to five or six feet wide at the bottom. The banks were topped with gorse faggots, packed flat and with the prickly side facing inwards, and all access points to the warren were fitted with closely shutting gates, each mounted upon a wooden sill so that the rabbits were unable to burrow their way underneath. Fortifications such as these created an almost insuperable barrier, even to the resourceful rabbit.

Close by stood the lonely and remote Warren Lodge, and it was here that Herbert Turner arrived at the age of nine years. Herbert's father had taken up the post of warrener on the Elveden estate, and the family moved to the lodge from their previous home in Hampshire. Herbert and his brother Jimmy were to remain at Elveden for the rest of their lives, Herbert as a warrener and then as a gamekeeper. Before he died in 1985, Herbert remembered how the warren looked in the days of his boyhood.

'Where the runways are today was acres and acres of bracken, sedge grass and what we call 'galls', patches of sand of about two or three acres. The rabbits ate all the grasses and everything else bar the bracken. As for trees, well there wasn't a tree on the whole heath, which probably ran into two thousand acres or more. The trees never stood a chance, and the rabbits ate the trees off like they did the grass.'

Before the Great War there were thirty warreners employed by the Elveden estate Game Department, and their job was to harvest the rabbits by shooting, trapping, snaring and ferreting. The number of rabbits taken off Elveden was quite enormous – in the first full season after the 1914–18 war 81,000 were shot, trapped and netted, and the following two seasons yielded 128,856 and 123,928 respectively. A good warrener could kill three or even four dozen in a day, as Herbert recalled:

'When we struck out onto the heathlands in the morning, there'd be a gang of us, about five in the gang, and you'd have your eye on one burrow, but you had to keep your position in the line as you went across the heath. If you got out of line you'd be stealing someone else's good burrow full of rabbits, and that wouldn't be fair!

'I would take a dog and a ferret and go ahead of my father, putting nets over the holes, then he'd come along behind me and he'd bolt out what he could with the ferrets into the nets and kill them.'

Those rabbits which were not bolted in the initial mêlée would hole up in the warren and had to be located by means of a line ferret, generally an experienced male or 'hob' ferret which was fitted with a 'coop' or muzzle, a collar and a long line.

'You'd take a ferret on a line with a collar around its neck and put that in the burrow. Eventually that'd catch the rabbit and kill it. In doing so that'd be making a noise, so you'd be listening on the ground, or your dog would, and you'd dig that out exactly down to where the noise was coming from. Sometimes you'd get two or even more, and if you had a good place you were well away for the day.'

A good warrener would know almost instinctively where to dig. As a guide he had only the ferret's line, marked each yard with a knot, but by striking his digging staff into the ground and pressing his ear to the end of it, he would hear the tell-tale scratching of the ferret or the movement of the rabbit. Then to check that he was over the right spot, he would lie on the ground and listen with an ear pressed to the earth – a ferreting skill which has all but vanished with the advent of the modern electronic bleeper.

Luckily the land around Elveden is light and sandy, so digging was not a difficult job. The warreners used the traditional digging staff, seven feet six inches in length and fitted with a spade at one end and a hook at the other to pick up the ferret line from an opened warren. Rarely, though, would a warrener need to go down more than three or four feet in depth. The warreners had great pride in their work, and when both ferret and rabbit had been removed, the hole was filled in and the turf replaced and trodden down so that it would be almost impossible to tell where the hole had been.

The months between October and March were what was termed the 'killing season', and this was the warrener's busiest time of the year. The warren could be a cold, bleak place during the winter, and to protect themselves from the elements the men wore a heavy smock.

'The real old rabbit catchers all had what we called smocks. That was a stout stuff what took a lot of work to make into these smock things, and they were looped around the neck and brought down just below the knee. They were tough, and you could be out practically all day in rain or snow or anything like that and you wouldn't get wet. They gave good shelter, especially when you used to have to lay on the ground and listen to the ferrets underneath the earth'.

When ferreting out on the warren, the warrener would mostly use purse nets, small circular nets fitted with draw strings and pegged over the entrances to the burrow. When the rabbit bolted into the net, the draw string would close behind it, trapping the rabbit and allowing the warrener to despatch it. But when dealing with rabbits alongside or within the game coverts, then a long net was called for. Made of knotted hemp, the long net was a hundred yards long and three and a half feet high. It was held in position by thin sticks pushed into the ground, and it was set at night around the perimeter of a covert, next to a field in which the rabbits were feeding.

'You'd bring your nets and creep along at about ten o'clock in the evening, especially if that were a nice breezy night. And you'd set these nets along between the rabbits and the woods, very quietly. You'd just creep about – we'd put the sticks up with not a word, hang our net up and keep going until that was all done.

'Then someone had to stay there all night to keep the nets clear and to take the rabbits out if any got in. Hedgehogs used to be a terrible nuisance if they got in and you couldn't get them out. They were so prickly to handle, you didn't know what to do.'

Once every few days the rabbit skin collectors would cycle from Lakenheath and Brandon to the outlying villages and to the farms and cottages, collecting the skins which had been hung out to dry. Thousand upon thousand of these skins were collected, and they formed the raw material for a trade unique to the breckland, the fur trade, which came to the area in the late eighteenth century and grew to a position of some considerable importance in the local economy. At one time most of the population of Brandon was engaged in 'furriering', working at or for one of the two old-established local factories which produced high quality felt hats.

After collecting several hundred thousand dried rabbit skins from warreners, gamekeepers and village folk, the skin merchants would sell their wares to one of the buyers from Brandon, the centre of the furriering business. Once at the factory the skins were sorted, graded and stripped of their coarse guard hairs to expose the soft under-fur that the hat trade required; this was then cut carefully away from the skin. Before mechanisation this job was undertaken by dozens of outworkers who first plucked the coat by hand, then removed the undercoat with sheep shears. But during the nineteenth century, machines were developed which shaved the rabbit skins much more cleanly than the old sheep shears, and produced a soft, even roll of fur ready for the felting process.

Blown under pressure by steam into a cylindrical drum fitted with wooden rollers, the fur was whirled round and round in a dense fog. Pounded, pummelled and pressed into submission by the rollers, it eventually congealed into a felted mat which was shrunk to the correct size for 'blocking' or forming into hats. These were then dyed brown, green, black or whatever colour was desired. Thus were created both the gentleman's bowler and the gamekeeper's billycock, and the fur trade flourished until the fashion for hats started to decline. Even then it might have remained a part of the breckland scene had it not been for myxomatosis, which dealt a death blow to the local rabbit population, and left the way open for Luton's wool felt manufacturers who took over the hat business.

The Brandon hat industry was a classic example of a local trade that was set up to make use of a natural resource, a trade which knitted into the village economy to provide valuable employment to all. From the warrener to the skin merchant, from the outworkers to the shearers, hatters and finishers, all benefited from the breckland bunny in one of those self-sustaining economic cycles that were at the core of pre-industrial England, and yet which today are scarce-remembered in snatches by old men.

Nothing went to waste. Even the rabbit skins, shorn of their fur and shredded by the stripping machines, were sold to the glue manufacturers and used to produce a glue which was highly prized by the aircraft factories in the 1914–18 war. And as for the heads, ears and legs – well, they went to produce the biggest cabbages in the whole of Brandon.

Working alone on the breck, the warreners were privileged to see a wonderful range of wild birds and animals, some of which have all but disappeared today: stone curlews, wheatears, shrikes that skewered their prey on thorny larders, pigeons nesting down rabbit holes, which the youngsters would try to catch with their purse nets; redstarts, linnets and goldcrests. Herbert Turner's particular favourites, however, were the crossbills which lived amongst the pine trees of the forestry plantations.

'They're lovely to watch. They hang underneath the branches of a Scots pine and feed on the deal-apple seeds, as we call them. They all hang underneath, and they have a lovely red tinge on the feathers. I think they're outstanding birds. And in the evening time you heard plenty of nightjars. One used to come on a dead branch just above the hut door, purring all night . . . but they're rare, if not gone now.'

At harvest time, the warrener's place was behind the reaper. Around the field he would walk with gun and dog, while the horses toiled in the hot August sunshine, the corn falling in golden swathes to be loosely bunched and stooked by the farmhands. As the corn went down, so the rabbits would bolt for the hedgerow, running the gauntlet of guns, dogs and any young lad from the village who fancied arming himself with a stick.

'We used to have to attend all the corn cutting to shoot the rabbits and hares, and with a bit of luck you might get a fox as well. But that used to be fun. After all, if you went out and shot fifty rabbits, that did very little to the rabbit population. I always wished that we could kill every rabbit we could get at, that was what we was for. We had all the cartridges we wanted, and we had a lot of fun.'

Fun was not the word used by one of the gentlemen invited to shoot at one of the rabbit drives for which Elveden was famous. The occasion in question was a shoot organised by Thomas Turner, head keeper at Elveden until 1953 and in his day one of the most celebrated keepers in Britain. Turner had planned to drive a covert called the Willows, a block of spruce which was then some twenty years old but only shallow rooted upon thin, stony soil – a recent gale had ripped through the covert and in consequence many of the trees had fallen or were leaning precariously against their neighbours. So the five Guns lined up one heavy, dank November morning, and the beaters took their places in readiness for the drive; and no sooner had Turner positioned the Guns and explained to them the layout of the drive than the first rabbits started coming across the line.

Very soon the shooting became a continuous bombardment. Loaders were cramming in cartridges as fast as they possibly

Gorse cutting on the warren

could, rabbits were dashing hither and thither in their hundreds and before long the guns were becoming too hot to hold. On top of it all, the beaters were going berserk, hollering, yelling and hitting out at the rabbits with their sticks. Every so often one of the uprooted trees would receive a charge of shot and down it would crash, adding to the general air of pandemonium, and the heavy atmosphere was thick with powder smoke. 'What anyone standing outside and not knowing what was really going on would have thought of it, I cannot imagine. It might easily have seemed as if a fierce private war had started', wrote Thomas Turner afterwards. It seems that eventually one of the Guns came up to him.

'Which is the nearest way out of this **** covert, Turner?' he gasped. The head keeper gave him the directions required, but reminded the guest that the party was to have one more drive before lunch. 'Drive be ****', he replied. 'I'm not staying one second longer in that **** inferno, neither do I intend finishing up today on a hook in your **** game larder.'

Surprisingly, neither beaters nor Guns sustained any injury, unless it were from a falling tree, but it must have been a close-run thing and was a pointed illustration of just how dangerous rabbit shooting could be. Particularly as these were highly experienced Guns who could keep their heads under conditions of the most extreme excitement – what would have happened if a party of lesser mortals had been shooting that day does not bear thinking about. Almost four hundred rabbits were killed in forty minutes by five Guns during the course of the drive that day – though nothing would ever induce that one Gun to set foot inside the Willows again.

By the eve of World War II a significant change had been wrought over the landscape and economy of the breckland. Penal levels of taxation, coupled with an agricultural depression in the 1920s, had forced a number of local estates to the brink of bankruptcy. There was no money in farming during the twenties, and even less money in farmland, especially when it was the light, hungry land of the breck. Then along came the Forestry Commission. Formed in 1919 with the expressed intention of providing Britain with a strategic supply of timber against the possibility of future conflict, the commission started an intensive programme of planting in the district. Culford, Brandon Park, Santon Downham and Mildenhall estates all disappeared under thickets of young pine and spruce trees, and slowly the landscape changed. The gnarled and blasted Scots pines, straggling across the breckland skyline in their rows and clumps as they had done for more than a century, were joined by huge, brooding blocks of conifers.

In the late 1930s the agricultural depression came to an end as Britain woke up to the threat of war, and once more the farming community geared itself up for food production. Naturally, this involved stepping up the fight against the rabbit, which came to be regarded not so much as a potentially useful economic asset, but more as the number one agricultural pest, to be destroyed by every means at the command of man. Then the military arrived. Elveden had seen the army before when in 1915 the estate had been used as a testing ground for the new tanks which the generals had hoped would bring an end to the stalemate of the trenches. They didn't, of course, and Thomas Turner had watched ruefully as his rabbit fences were demolished by the cumbersome beasts.

Now it was the American air force which took up residence. The famous war memorial which stands next to the main Norwich to Newmarket road, and which had been built by Lord Iveagh in memory of those from Elveden, Icklingham and Eriswell who fell in the Great War, became a lookout for American observers. United States servicemen were

stationed in Elveden Hall, and Lakenheath warren was bought by compulsory purchase and turned into an aerodrome; where Warren Lodge stood, the control tower of the new air base was sited. Yet the engineers did not destroy the old landmarks entirely. In particular they left the cottage garden of the lodge and the vegetable patch which the old warreners and their wives had lovingly tended, together with its three greengage trees which Herbert had climbed as a boy. All over the estate, the land was enclosed for farming. Former heaths which had seen nothing but rabbits and a few sheep were earmarked for agricultural production and converted to arable farming.

In 1938 Harry Kent Woolsey joined the Elveden staff as a rabbit catcher. Harry was born nearby at Brandon and his father had a farm at Thetford. Before coming to Elveden Harry, like many other local men, had worked for the Forestry Commission. According to Harry:

'There were half a dozen warreners on the estate in those days. Even then, it wasn't like it had been in the twenties, although I suppose there were just as many rabbits about. In the beginning you couldn't grow anything. You could stand there and see the corn being eaten off, and the next day that would be eaten off a little further. There were rabbits everywhere. In some places I could shoot twenty or thirty rabbits without moving, and I used to get hundreds out of a cornfield.'

Warrens and sheepwalks formed the mainstay of the old breckland community

Rabbit fencing became a top priority amongst the warreners. A block of land newly selected for improvement would be fenced, planted with shelter belts of Scots pine and then systematically cleared of rabbits. Elveden didn't order rabbit wire by the yard, it ordered it by the mile. One order alone was for fifty miles of wire, and the estate formed a wiring squad to carry out the job of rabbit fencing. Naturally the warreners then had to patrol the fences regularly to stop up any holes, an arduous and time-consuming task from which there was no let-up, summer or winter.

The key to much of the reclamation work was the cutting of a new relief channel around the western perimeter of the Elveden estate. For centuries, the land around the neighbouring village of Wangford had remained a boggy wilderness, the haunt of wildfowl, otters, spectacular butterflies and rare marsh plants. But once drained, the black, peaty soil brought forth bounty of a more agricultural nature.

Much of the land was put down to lucerne on a five year rotation. Thousands of acres were managed like this as grazing for cattle, but in due course the land also produced good crops of cereals. Rye in particular has always enjoyed the light, sandy land, and much of it continues to be grown in the district to this day. The cattle are now long gone and there is no dairying on the estate any more. Harry's main job now is protecting crops.

'Wherever there's any sign of a rabbit, that's my job to get rid of it. We shoot, trap and snare, and we do a lot of gassing with Cymag, but that's terrible stuff. You've got to be so careful with it, 'cos that's a real killer. I first used it with the rabbit clearance people in '61. Two of you always have to be together whenever you are using gas, and you have to have the antidote with you. If not, and you get a whiff of it, you're in real trouble.

'I've gassed rabbits with a spoon, put it down the hole, and a rabbit has shot out three or four yards and then dropped dead. Very often I've done that. Some say you should wear a mask, but I don't because it's not practical. Get a little Cymag on a mask and you're dead. It's much better to let the gas blow away.'

Harry is much happier using traps and snares. He runs twenty traps and sixty snares at a time, all of which have to be visited daily. The snares are bought, but Harry makes the pegs, and also the 'tealer' or 'pricker' with which each snare is fitted in order to hold it at just the correct distance off the ground, the height of a rabbit's head as it scuttles through its grassy run.

'I snare on the runs, in the grass. That's a good way to catch rabbits and the snares are cheap to buy. They last me a year, and I get through a fair few snares.' On two separate occasions, Harry has caught two rabbits in the same snare. In each case a doe had got herself caught in the snare and had subsequently been approached by an amorous buck that had succeeded only in getting himself tangled up in the wire. And several times, Harry has had a snared rabbit killed by a clever stoat which has followed the line of snares each morning, thereby finding himself an easy meal.

As for traps, Harry considers that the modern Juby trap, though much more humane, is not nearly so effective at catching rabbits as the old gin trap: 'It's the size of these Juby traps that's the problem. You set the traps and it's perhaps a week before the rabbits will come into them. It's all on account of your having to cut a hole big enough to get the trap in, because the trap itself is so big and the jaws open so wide. As soon as you disturb the hole, the rabbits don't like it.'

Shooting is also one of the principal control methods used at Elveden, and the Guns still go out at harvest time to walk behind the combine. These days, however, there are far fewer rabbits in the corn than ever there used to be, for modern herbicides mean that the bottom of the crop is now so clean that there is nothing there for a rabbit to live on. But it is still very much part of a traditional scene, in the parched heat of a breckland summer, the corn glowing white in the August sun and a distant belt of Scots pine dancing and shimmering in the haze. On a dusty track along the field margin, bounded by bracken and purple willow herb, the yellowhammer calls for his 'little bit of bread and no cheese', gorse pods snap in the heat, meadow browns and gatekeepers flop drowsily around the field margin and a lark trills upward into the wide sky.

Then with a roar and a snort, the combine enters the field, with a tractor and trailer in attendance to cart the corn straight back to the grain store. Walking alongside are Harry and one of the keepers, who both line out in a strategic position as the machine starts its circuit of the field. Within minutes the first rabbit is bolting for the hedgerow and safety, but with the swing of the professional Harry tracks it with his gun, a bang is heard above the noise of the combine and the bunny bowls head over heels to lie still in the stubble.

'I go in behind the combines, but once round and that's about it. In the old days there used to be plenty of rabbits in there, before the corn was sprayed properly, but they've changed, have the rabbits. They now lay on top of the land much more than they used to.

'Now I try to control them with night shooting, in the evenings with a shotgun – a rifle is too dodgy with so many people about. Before it gets completely dark I go out with the

keepers in a van and we shoot by the headlights. That's a good way of controlling rabbits – I reckon I get six out of ten, and that's good sport as well.'

The big change in the business of rabbit control came about with the advent of myxomatosis. This vile disease was introduced artificially in the early 1950s, and within a few years the rabbit population of the breckland was virtually wiped out. Where once the heaths were a moving sea of bobtails, there remained but a few piteous rabbits, their eyes hideously distorted and their senses dulled to the point of extinction. And round about lay the bleaching bones of their fellows, thousand upon thousand of them, mouldering in sickly smelling, maggot-ridden piles of carrion that were of use only to the crow, the magpie and the fox. Yet amazingly the rabbit survived, albeit in much reduced numbers, and these days the population fluctuates from year to year, as Harry explains:

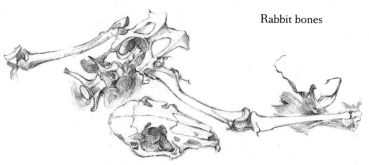

Rabbit bones

'Myxomatosis is the main thing that controls the rabbits nowadays. We haven't had it badly for a couple of years and so the numbers are up again, and it's the numbers of rabbits that governs the disease – when the rabbits increase then the myxie comes back. You don't see the myxie so much in the winter or springtime, it seems to come back more in the summer when there are more rabbits about.'

Not surprisingly, the advent of myxomatosis spelt the end to the trade in rabbit meat for human consumption. Even today, country people are still wary about eating wild rabbit, while the butchers and game dealers compound the ultimate indignity by importing frozen rabbit meat from overseas. Locally harvested wild rabbits are worth only pennies to the dealer, and they are not even paunched before they are committed to the freezer. Most of them end up as dog food, the tinned variety with 'rabbit flavour'.

Furthermore, the decimation of the rabbit population has led to wholesale changes in the breckland environment, so much so that local conservationists now fear for some of the region's traditional species – for where once the heaths were cropped short by a million pairs of incisors, now gorse, scrub and undergrowth flourishes. Deer have found the new conditions to their liking and are on the increase, especially red, roe and the tiny muntjac deer, but breckland rarities like the stone curlew are fast disappearing; ironically the local landowners are now being encouraged to fence what remains of the ancient heaths and to employ sheep to graze them back to their former condition. There is even talk in some quarters of reintroducing rabbits, though this is something that the local landowners find it hard to countenance; certainly it is something that Harry Kent Woolsey could never accept. After a lifetime spent trying to destroy rabbits, he remains their implacable enemy:

'Rabbit catching, well that's a regular job. They're a proper pest, I kill one and there's ten more. I haven't killed the last one yet, and I don't suppose I ever shall. But I'm working on it.'

LEFT
Harry Kent Woolsey

Reaching for a high wigeon

THE
SHOOTING HUT

As they move up and down the washes, the wigeon can darken the sky. And when you have waited since long before sunrise, crouched knee-deep in the floodwater against a drunken gatepost, the arrival of such a congregation of wildfowl out of a fenland dawn is an experience never to be forgotten.

Standing at the head of the wash, beneath a clump of gnarled old willow trees, and sheltered by the Hundred Foot bank from the keen east wind which knifes across the bare fen landscape, stands the shooting hut. Acting as a repository for hides, poles, tools, bags of barley and the other impedimenta which are required for the efficient running of an inland duck shoot, it has long become the focal point of our small marsh.

From within its modest but homely walls many a fowler has ventured forth into the freezing gloom of a January dawn and to them he has returned, tired and cold, for a mug of steaming soup or a welcome bite to eat. And on a winter's evening, when wildfowl movement on the marsh has long since slackened to a bare trickle, its timbers have echoed to the sound of jovial banter and wildfowling yarns till far into the night.

Many weighty matters have been discussed in wildfowling huts, among which the 'Black Hut' at Patrington Haven on the north shore of the Humber estuary is perhaps the most famous. That celebrated structure was the headquarters of a man who many consider the father of modern wildfowling, Stanley Duncan. Engineer, railway worker and gun-shop proprietor, he founded the Wildfowlers' Association of Great Britain and Ireland, forerunner of today's British Association for Shooting and Conservation.

Inside the tarred and salt-stained weatherboards of the Black Hut, Duncan and his companions mulled over the problems which faced their sport at the turn of the century and sowed the germ of a national wildfowling organisation. Even in those distant times there were fears amongst shooting folk over the loss of marshes, the decline in wildfowl populations and the difficulties facing the dwindling number of professional gunners who plied the estuaries and wetlands of Britain.

The Black Hut remained beside the Humber for many years, a monument to Stanley Duncan and his dream of a guardian organisation for the shooting man, until finally it succumbed to wind and tide, ending up as a sad pile of driftwood on the shoreline.

Many years later, as part of the BASC's seventy-fifth anniversary celebrations, the Hull and East Riding Wildfowlers' Association helped organise a magnificent exhibition about the life and times of Stanley Duncan. The centrepiece was a loving reconstruction of the hut itself, complete with much of Duncan's original wildfowling gear. And what a marvellous and evocative reconstruction it was, too. It seemed as if, at any moment, the great man himself might have emerged, swathed in calico and oilskins, a great double eight bore over his arm and a brace of curlews slung across his shoulder.

Our own hut on the Hundred Foot washes, close to the border of Norfolk and Cambridgeshire, may have had something of a more modest history, though it too has seen its portals darkened by some of wildfowling's noted figures. And its birth was hardly less romantic.

When the wash was purchased, back in the very early nineteen seventies, it was soon realised that a base was needed for fowling operations. In those days a two or three day wildfowling trip meant booking into the Lamb and Flag in the nearby village of Welney, complete with dogs, guns, muddy waders, evil-smelling Barbours and all. Not that any of us had anything against the Lamb and Flag; indeed Roy, the genial landlord, welcomed shooters with open arms, turning a blind eye to dogs in the bedrooms and worrying not a jot about the comings and goings at unearthly hours. And in the evenings we could toast our feet beside a roaring fire and sup pints of Elgoods ale in a bar bedecked with punt gun and monster pike.

Such was the benefit of staying at the Lamb and Flag. The drawback came in the early hours of the morning, when it was time to make the arduous trek across the washes to Welney suspension bridge, then up and along the Hundred Foot bank. The journey was a fair enough proposition in the early part of the season, when a cross country vehicle could mount the bank and carry its occupants in comfort, more or less, the couple of miles to their destination. In really dry weather even a family saloon might tackle the trip, though the wise driver would avoid leaving his car on any section of the bank to which the Welney bullocks had access – those beasts are furnished with tongues like rasps that have been known to strip the paint clean off a Morris Minor.

Nowadays the ascent of the bank has been eased by means of generous helpings of hardcore, though it is still a fair test for most four wheel drive vehicles. Twenty years ago the bank was treacherous to the point of real danger, and on more than one occasion did the Land-Rover slither down it, sideways, to within inches of a bottomless dyke. In the depths of winter, when the rutted bank top tracks churned into liquid mud and became impassable to anything larger than a trials bike, there was nothing for it but to trust one's luck to a small boat across the Hundred Foot River, or to slog it down the bank on foot.

The former course of action involved launching a fibreglass dinghy in the pitch darkness down a near-vertical slope into the swirling, muddy torrent of the Hundred Foot River. Add to that frail craft a couple of robust wildfowlers, their guns, cartridge bags, hides, lunch boxes, several sacks of decoys and a brace of over-excited dogs and there was a recipe for almost certain disaster. Two of our syndicate were virtually brought up in small boats along the north Norfolk coast and cut their teeth on the Atlantic convoys, yet even they placed lives and property at risk when put in command of a dinghy across those thirty five yards of treacherous water. The footsloggers' option, meanwhile, spelled a nerve-racking dash across what must surely be the busiest railway bridge in the east of England followed by a twenty-five minute hike along the bank, borne down with every conceivable item of fowling gear.

It starts to become clear why we agreed that some convenient headquarters, sited upon the marsh itself and which could at a pinch sleep two or more wildfowlers, had obvious advantages. On one memorable occasion we went as far as pitching a two-man tent to act as base camp during an extended trip to the washes. It was January and the marsh was three parts flooded, with a hard freeze in prospect. For two nights the snow drifted over our flysheet while the biting wind tugged at the guy ropes and threatened every moment to wrench the tent pegs clean out of the ground – indeed it must surely have done so had they not been firmly frozen into the peat.

Emerging from the zippered cocoon at first light we must have looked like refugees from Scott's last expedition, and though the tent itself proved quite warm enough, there were real difficulties when it came to trying to prevent the icy wind from blowing out our primus stove as the evening meal of bangers and beans was prepared. Camping was clearly not the long-term solution.

So more grandiose plans were formulated. A hut was what we needed, and during the course of the following spring the materials with which to construct one were gathered together. Ted Eales, one of our six-man syndicate, was warden at the National Trust reserve at Blakeney Point in north Norfolk. In those days Ted worked closely with my father, then a producer with Anglia Television. He was a natural wildlife cameraman,

Across the flooded marsh

shooting the most wonderful and evocative material at Blakeney and elsewhere. The two of them would spend days up on the Point during the summer filming the terns for which Blakeney was famous, and I would join them during the school holidays. When the conditions were not suitable for photography, Ted collected driftwood, of which there was an endless supply washed up along the beach after every big tide. Each timber ship which disgorged part of its load into the North Sea added to the steadily growing pile of planks gleaned from the tideline.

Every few days Ted took his ancient Massey Ferguson along the foot of the dunes, scouring the high tide mark for timber. Sometimes there was none, but on other occasions the back of the tractor was loaded so high that the front barely touched the ground. So it was that Sue, Ted's old springer spaniel, had a lucky break when, running beside the moving vehicle, she turned and dived straight under the front wheels. Instead of killing her instantly, the tractor rode up over the surprised spaniel and Sue emerged shaken but unscathed.

In summer the washes provide rich grazing for cattle

By July there was sufficient timber stacked in the sandy yard behind the old lifeboat house for construction to commence, and the three of us, Ted, my father and I, set about the task of building our hut. It was to be made in five sections – four walls and a massively heavy floor. Each plank was cut to size and nailed into place and slowly, over the course of a weekend, the hut took shape. The sections were loosely bolted together and openings made to take the windows and door. For our main window Ted had salvaged the split windscreen of an old Land-Rover, while a second window frame was unearthed from the junk and rummage which, with the sand and wild lupins, gave that yard its own very special character.

On the evening of the second day the hut was complete. Carefully the bolts, windows and door were removed and the sections roped together on the back of the tractor. The following morning we were up early to catch the tide. The beach which fringes Blakeney harbour is just a few hundred yards from the old lifeboat house where we were staying, and slowly, gingerly, the old tractor bore its load down through the dunes, along the shingle bank which marks the top of the beach, then down over the firm sand to the water's edge. The tide was making fast as we manhandled the hut sections onto the sand, and within twenty minutes they were well afloat and ready for the next lap of their journey.

Fixing a tow rope around the bobbing timbers, Ted brought up his powerful motor launch, hitched the spare end of the tow rope around one of the stern posts, pointed the bows towards the squat, distant tower of Morston church and opened the throttle. With a surge of power the hut sections gurgled and bubbled, spewing flecks of foam before lurching forwards and skidding across the tops of the waves like a giant surfboard. Twenty minutes later we were edging up Morston creek to where Ted had positioned a mighty boat trailer, onto which the hut was soon floated and hauled clear of the water. A few days later it was loaded into a furniture van for the final stage of its journey, across Norfolk to Welney and the Hundred Foot washes.

Ever since that day, furniture van drivers have had my utmost admiration. The timid suggestion that he might be able to get his vehicle up the Hundred Foot bank and thus save us from having to float the hut sections one by one across yet another river, was accepted by the driver not merely as an instruction, but as a direct challenge to man and machine. Far from taking one look at the greasy gradient, dumping his load at the roadside and hightailing it back to Norwich, our driver summoned up his not inconsiderable courage, took a run at the bank and at the third attempt conquered it. Within forty minutes the hut had arrived, more or less intact, at its appointed site on a bank of spoil thrown up to stand clear of everything but the very worst of winter floods.

Reassembly was a relatively straightforward job. By the end of the first day we had got the floor, walls, door and windows into position and added a roof of tongued and grooved matchboarding, a job lot that had been sold off cheaply by a local timber merchant because it had got wet and stained in storage. By this stage of the proceedings, a few blue marks on the ceiling were the last thing likely to cause us any concern.

The roof was topped off with a layer of good thick bitumen felt. Then the walls, too, were felted and painted with one of Ted's own special concoctions based on grey Admiralty paint, leavened with just about every shade of grey, green and brown you can imagine. The result might have appeared somewhat unconventional, but it was certainly effective, both as a protective coating against the ravages of the fenland winter and as a camouflage to soften the hut's stark outline.

Finally a series of larchwood laths were fixed to the walls in order to hold the felt firmly in place, and the hut was finished. Three prouder wildfowlers one could not imagine as we stood back to admire our handiwork and ponder on the sheer graft and effort which it represented. Who would have thought that this squat, workmanlike structure, nestling so naturally into the Hundred Foot bank, had been born on a beach fifty miles away and had travelled by land and sea to its final resting place? Only the unmistakable tang of salt in the timber betrayed the hut's true origins.

Now the Land-Rover screen faced out across the washes, giving a panoramic view across our marsh and enabling a fowler to watch the flighting wigeon or see the teal dropping down into our flight pond as he finished his mid-morning snack and planned the afternoon's sport. Camp beds were lined up along the walls, jars of tea, sugar and the foul tasting powdered milk which Ted insisted upon drinking were stacked on the shelf, and a paraffin heater was installed. Come the turn of the year and the warm glow of a September sun across the fens, and it would be time for our new headquarters to see service.

The writer outside the shooting hut

The first frosts of autumn bring the fowl to the washes in their thousands. From Scandinavia and northern Russia they come: teal, mallard, and pintail in small trips which whicker in on set wings at evening flight or arrive under the golden orb of the hunter's moon. But the glory, the spectacle of the washes are its wigeon. Rising and falling in countless numbers, the great flocks lift from the silver floodwaters to settle elsewhere on fresh grazing and fill the wide bowl of the fenland sky with their wild whistling. As they move up and down the washes, now in a great battalion two thousand strong, now splitting into innumerable little groups of twenty, ten or half a dozen, the Welney wigeon can indeed darken the sky. And when you have waited since long before sunrise, crouched knee-deep in the floodwater against a drunken gatepost, the arrival of such a congregation of wildfowl out of the ruddy glow of a fenland dawn is an experience never to be forgotten.

In a moment there are ducks all about you, wild duck, newly returned from the high Arctic; pack after pack of them pirouetting down with paddles set, others quartering past while, high above, yet more wigeon circle as they wait their turn to settle on the favoured wash, their wings and whistles filling the air with sound. Maybe you fire three or four shots, sending wigeon or mallard spinning down to splash into the water beside you. More likely you just gaze in wonder. There is time enough for flight shooting when the ducks are moving in a steady stream of twos and threes: to fire when such a flock is around you is to break a spell, to halt a moment of magic.

It is a rare treat to find yourself amongst such a crowd of wild ducks; striking a day when weather and birds combine to produce top quality sport may on the other hand come once or twice a season to the diligent wildfowler. Pencilled on the wall of the shooting hut is the record of just such a day. Or more properly three days. For the mixed bag of wildfowl and waders listed in a spidery hand on the peeling paintwork was made on one of the first big fowling expeditions to be based in the new hut.

It was December and the washes were flooded and frozen, great sheets of ice locking the reeds and marsh grass in an iron grip. I was seventeen years old at the time and the three of

Flight time against the winter willows

us, Ted Eales, my father and I, had shot evening flight with some success; but the ducks had flighted late, and the sky had been too clear to see them easily against the darkness of a winter's dusk. As night fell, and with the sound of wings still whistling overhead, we had returned to the hut.

Long into the evening we yarned by the guttering light of a gas lamp, cleaning guns as the dogs groomed themselves and curled up into their respective corners. Then it was time to set out the camp beds, and as the lamp finally dimmed it was to a cosy jumble of fowlers, sleeping bags, dogs and shooting gear all competing for whatever space was available.

The following morning the alarm sounded well before daybreak. A light powdering of snow had fallen during the night, and the rank grasses crunched under our waders as we headed for the Delph River, some three quarters of a mile distant. A pair of mallard called out of the gloom, rising from a flowing dyke that had remained open throughout the freeze, while a snipe zig-zagged away into the purple fingers which heralded the coming of dawn, scaap-scaaping furiously.

Apart from the sound of distant ducks and the far off trumpeting of a herd of Bewick's swans all was silent. Not a breath of wind shook the rushes around the edges of my hide. It is mornings such as these, long before the world is awake and about its business, that repay all the the hard work and effort of wildfowling. Just to see the long crystals of rime on the reed heads glint pink with the first flush of light from the east makes one put aside all thoughts of cold toes or frozen fingers. It is as though a glorious celestial slide show of coloured light is being put on just for you – mauve, salmon pink, apple green and peach; each tint lasting for just a few seconds as the sun moves ever closer to the horizon.

Then in a flash a pair of teal zip by. The shot is miles behind, but not so the next, which connects with a high cock wigeon, quartering out of the dawn, the early light picking out the pink feathers of his breast. A thump in the grass and the dog is out in an instant to make the retrieve. Morning flight has started.

Small parties of wigeon make their way down the washes, coming out of the north east, and as they do so a bank of shower clouds appears below them on the horizon, the tops picked out in gold against the clear sky. The wigeon turn and curl downwards into a light breeze which is already rustling the frosted grass, offering the challenge of a shot.

Soon a variety of chances had put half a dozen birds in the bag, mostly wigeon, but also a single teal which had skimmed the line of hides like a driven grouse. It was now clear that the snow showers which had been forecast were but a few miles away. Towering out of the north east came the squall clouds, brilliantly lit by the morning sun yet with their bases dark and pregnant with snow. As the first flurry of flakes arrived, the wind rose from a gentle zephyr to a gusting breeze which tugged at the hide and stung the face. Suddenly the ducks were on the move. Unsettled by the sudden squall they lifted and moved up and down the washes, peeling off into small groups which battled into the snow showers.

In winter the washes are a stark but beautiful place of flood and frost

We all shot well that morning. Each time a snow squall blew up out of the north east there was a frenetic burst of activity from the fowl and a spell of exciting shooting which ceased almost as soon as the shower clouds passed and the sun came out. I have often found that the wildfowl on the washes behave in this way, moving in the teeth of a squall of wind, rain or snow, then settling again once the weather has calmed, and over the years I have experienced some of my most memorable days under such conditions. On this occasion the showers continued until around midday, when, laden with heavy game bags, we returned to the hut for a welcome mug of soup.

By then the clouds had receded towards the distant horizon and a more general veil of grey was creeping across the sky, dimming the brilliance of the low winter sun and heralding a change in the weather. For several weeks before the freeze, our wash had been fed regularly with tail barley. Bucketfuls of the stuff had been tipped into the wet flashes which dotted the marsh, and now that barley was locked into the ice. With the thaw, however, would come the ducks, eager for an easy meal.

Late that afternoon we took the Land-Rover along the bank and into Littleport, where, at a small agricultural merchant, we purchased the supplies which would enable us to put into train a two-phase operation designed to capitalise upon the change in the weather: two bags of industrial salt and a hundred and fifty cartridges. Phase one was to involve scattering the salt over our icebound wash – this was Ted's idea, and a brilliant one it was, too. He reasoned that with a bit of luck our wash would thaw overnight before any of the other neighbouring marshes, and by daybreak, hopefully, the ducks would have found the barley. Phase two would involve using the cartridges.

The hides had to be moved from their sites along the distant Delph to positions around our own flooded wash, for there would not be time for hide building before morning flight. By then with any luck the birds would already be pitching into the barley from all quarters and there would not be a moment to waste.

Phase one worked like a charm. The thaw came that evening and ours was the first wash to show open water. During the night, under the overcast sky, one could hear what seemed like dozens of mallard calling to each other, splashing and preening as they guzzled the tempting grain. The picture was confirmed in the first grey light of dawn. A persistent drizzle was now falling, and though most of the washes remained under an inch or more of ice, there were big open patches of water where the salt had been scattered.

Through the murk sideslipped ghostly shapes of mallard, planing in on set wings, then jinking as they realised their mistake. Sometimes they were too quick for the shot which scythed after them, but more often a plump duck somersaulted into the slush.

It was a memorable morning flight, and we packed up while the birds were still coming in, now beneath a glowering, leaden sky which spat down a drenching, penetrating rain. Back in the hut our three-day bag was sorted; fat-breasted mallard, bunches of wigeon, the cocks resplendent with chestnut heads fronted by a blaze of primrose yellow, pretty little teal, shoveler, gadwall, half a dozen succulent snipe, a couple of stray woodcock and a solitary woodpigeon which had chosen the wrong moment to make its flight across the washes. A tally fit to gladden the heart of any wildfowler.

Today the record of that expedition slowly fades on the weathered wooden walls. Since then much has happened to the hut. Floods have come and gone. Some of them left six inches or more of silt and mud on the wooden floor, and eventually the boards rotted and had to be replaced with concrete paving slabs. The original spartan interior was lined with fibreboard, then plywood, and the work of rot and rodent has necessitated the insertion of new structural timbers to keep the roof from sagging.

But the basic fabric remains, and so do the memories. Bunches of teal and wigeon hanging from imaginary hooks, sketched in oils on the wall. A half-forgotten game book sits on the shelf, with records of days spent out amongst the floodwaters still mouldering amongst its mouse-nibbled pages. Outside stands a rusting golf trolley once used to transport hides and decoys across the marsh, an ancient, decrepit grain bin, a motley collection of broken hide poles and discarded chicken wire. All sorts of wonders lurk behind that wicket gate which bears the legend 'No Hawkers or Circulars', and which with its barbed wire fence keeps the grazing cattle away from the hut.

And through that Land-Rover windscreen one can still gaze across the washes, scanning the sky for a flight line, waiting for the wigeon to move or marking the slow, steady beat of the marsh harrier quartering the fen. One day, no doubt, the hut will go the same way as did Stanley Duncan's, but with luck that day is still a long way off.

THE CALL OF
THE WILD

Jim Cracknell follows a family keepering tradition. He reckons that the first thing he must have set eyes on as a youngster was a gun standing in the corner of the parlour. With a lifetime of keepering in Suffolk, he is increasingly turning his attention towards encouraging wild game.

A winter snipe drive

Waiting in the reeds

There is a quiet revolution taking place in game shooting. A small number of influential sportsmen – for they are sportsmen first and shooters second – are rebelling against a trend which has afflicted low ground game shooting for more than a decade, the demand for larger and yet larger bags.

The 1980s saw what amounted to a re-run of that most unsubtle episode in the history of field sports, the indulgent and prodigious Edwardian shooting party. Powered by the engine of a buoyant economy, lubricated by big city bucks and steered by overt commercialism, a small but significant number of game shooters once again made the assumption that big is beautiful. Likewise a minority of shoots attempted to satisfy the aspirations of those who believed that new-found wealth, or the wheeling and dealing involved in its creation, needed the status which derived from the *grande battue*. Having made a killing in the city, people wanted also to make a killing in the countryside.

Once again the talk was of records and, appalling though it was, records were duly broken. Game farms churned out ever-increasing numbers of pheasants as more and more shoots released more and more birds, and the market price for shot game went through the floor. In 1989 there was even talk of dead game being buried on some estates, though nobody was willing to name names.

What was worse, some game shooters were prepared, perhaps because they knew no different, to accept poor quality shooting. A hundred overweight, farmed pheasants with all the aerobatic skills of a squadron of broiler house turkeys were kicked reluctantly into the air by teams of beaters, where once a dozen small, wily and nimble birds had accelerated high into the air and then twisted and curled over the Guns. But now the revolution is upon us, and the call is for quality rather than quantity, for genuinely wild game rather than the mass-produced products of the poultry farm, for a sustainable form of shooting which puts back into the countryside what it takes out and which balances the needs of game birds with the wider imperatives of wildlife conservation. The revolution has come not a moment too soon.

It is, of course, the shoot owners who ultimately decide how their sport is to be managed, whether they will spend yet more money on releasing yet more pheasants or whether instead they will accept smaller bags and move to a less intensive form of sport which relies upon a holistic approach to countryside management, where farming and game conservation work hand in hand and the traditional skills of the gamekeeper are ranked higher than his ability as a poultry farmer. But the keepers, too – at least those of the more old-fashioned sort – welcome the dawning of the move back to what they see as their proper role in life.

Jim Cracknell has been a gamekeeper for forty-five years, all of them in the county of Suffolk. He is now a head keeper in his thirty-fifth season on the same estate, Helmingham, the home of Lord Tollemache, a landowner who himself has made a positive decision to move towards wild game. Jim looks with disapproval at the new commercial shoots and the sort of gamekeeping which they engender:

'Well, I think that's the same with everything when money comes into it, that takes the sporting side right away. These fellows, they're there to kill birds. They aren't looking for the high ones, them old sporting birds; they won't let three or four go to get a good 'un. No, they just bang 'em down, because they've paid for so many.

'On these commercial shoots they rear thousands and thousands of birds. I mean there's some places where I hear them say "Don't worry about killing vermin, just rear an extra thousand pheasants to counteract it." Well, that isn't gamekeeping, is it? At least it isn't to me.'

Helmingham is an enclave of tradition in a part of England which, more than most, has been subject to the changes that have swept through the countryside over the last few decades. The southern and eastern counties, always the heartland of game shooting, were those most dramatically affected by the intensification of agriculture that reached its rapacious heights during the 1970s. Modern farming affected wild game survival in two fundamental ways: firstly, by removing hedges and field boundaries to accommodate ever larger machines, it took away the breeding and resting cover which all wild creatures require. And in doing so it isolated those populations which did remain by destroying their communications network, for hedgerows are the routes by which wildlife moves about the landscape. Secondly, chemical farming starved the gamebird chicks of the insect food which they need to sustain them in the first crucial weeks of life – not only do insecticides kill the aphids and bugs themselves, but herbicides eliminate the broad-leaved weeds on which the insects thrive. The overall result has been splendid crops of cereals, but fields which are almost entirely devoid of game and wildlife.

Sixty-three years old, Jim Cracknell started his gamekeeping career in his home village of Bruisyard, near Framlingham, after the last war. He joined the staff on the Earl of Stradbroke's estate at the age of nineteen and later worked as a gamekeeper at Cavenham, near Bury St Edmunds, before moving to Helmingham. As gamekeeper and countryman, he has seen the changes which were wrought across the East Anglian landscape with the advent of chemical agriculture, and watched the hedgerows disappear in Suffolk.

'Sprays: that's a deadly thing for the gamekeeper when you see that spray go round, deadly. Some of the farmers will even hang a spray boom over the hedge if you can't be there and have a word with them. That's your main bugbear, sprays.

'But some of the farmers are now starting to look after the hedges again. During the war and afterwards the government were giving you a grant to pull the hedges out to make the fields bigger, but now what are they doing today? They're now a-paying on 'em to put 'em back again! Well, that's a good thing for me. I like to see these hedges and headlands left.'

He is lucky at Helmingham. Five hundred years of owner-ship within the same family has ensured that change in this part of Suffolk is slow and measured, that it accords with the best principles of stewardship of the countryside. The estate is therefore run on traditional lines: tenanted farms, fields which average no more than twenty acres, ancient meadows set amongst the arable crops, and above all thick, deep hedge-rows with wide grassy banks in which the wild grey par-tridges can nest. For Jim has a love of his wild partridges which shines through as he walks the fields, meadows and hedgerows:

'The English partridges used to be a picture in the valleys around here when I first came to the estate. Of course in those days the partridges used to be nearly all grey, and that was marvellous to see them fly off the hills. You used to stand your guns fairly well back so that the birds would go over the hedge and lift again, and they used to go like a bomb-burst. Oh, that used to be a wonderful sight.'

It was an art to drive wild grey partridges, an art which was understood by only a limited number of gamekeepers and one which is now almost forgotten. For unlike the reared bird, the wild partridge was bonded to its own territory and could be driven for perhaps no more than a couple of fields before the coveys broke back over the heads of the beaters: 'Them old partridges would go so far and then say "No further, we're a-going back!" With these reared ones, you keep behind them and you can keep 'em a-going, 'cause they've got no home, they've got no anchor.'

Thanks largely to the work of the Game Conservancy, landowners and their gamekeepers now have the knowledge to restore the fortunes of the wild grey partridge. They know that they should leave a wide grassy bottom alongside their hedges and that they should operate a restricted spraying regime along the headlands. Such 'conservation headlands' are a feature of Jim's beat, and even in early spring, as the partridges pair up and seek out their nesting territories, you can see the broad-leaved weeds sprouting around the six metres of field closest to the hedge bank.

Jim is all in favour of the conservation headland technique, because he wins in two ways: his wild partridge chicks are supplied with an abundant supply of insect food, and the grain combined from along the headlands – which inevitably contains a certain amount of weed seed and is thus of reduced commercial value – is made available to the game department for use as pheasant food.

He also approves of the way that the majority of the hedges on the estate have been retained, in stark contrast to what has happened over much of Suffolk. In particular, he points to those hedge banks which enclose the traditional 'long meadows' that intersect the estate. Winding along the bottoms of the valleys, and with a tall hedge on either side, the meadows make ideal places in which to stand the guns when driving partridges. There are not many parts of East Anglia where the old permanent pastures have been retained – all too often they fell victim to the plough during the aggressive years of the 1970s. Where they do remain, the old grasslands are a delight to behold. In the spring they are a carpet of wild flowers: ladies' smock paints the lower, wetter meadows with delicate tints of mauve

and pink, while cowslips and primroses blossom under the hedgerows. And later, the pastures turn yellow with buttercups and luxuriate in the heady scent of meadowsweet.

Sympathetic management of farmland for the benefit of game has its cost, of course. The farmer does not profit from it at all, indeed, he has to forego some of the extra money which he could make were he to spray right up to the headlands, grub up the hedges and plough the old pastures. Where the farmer is also the landowner then at least he can enjoy the benefits of seeing more wild game about his farm, and perhaps gain extra pleasure from the shooting which it offers; thus sport provides a strong incentive for the maintenance of less intensive patterns of agriculture. Where he is a tenant, then of course it is up to his landlord to come to an agreement over the farming policy with respect to game. But nevertheless, the keeper must still use all of his tact and diplomacy.

'Never fall out with anybody if you can help it. Because once you make an enemy that's easy for him, if he sees a pheasant or a partridge nest, to put his foot in it. You've got to try and keep everybody happy and never treat any-one better than you do the next man. With tenant farmers, what you do for one, you've always got to remember to do for the other.'

ABOVE: Wild game for the table
LEFT: Jim Cracknell

Habitat management is central to the encouragement of wild game, but on the whole it is the territory of the farmer, landowner or farm manager rather than that of the game-keeper. The control of vermin, however, falls squarely into the keeper's court, and spring is the time when he must make his greatest effort to protect the nests and the young game birds from attack by predators.

'A lot of people think that once the shooting is over, then the gamekeeper's work has finished. But if a game-keeper don't work March, April, May and June, then he don't want to worry about next winter, 'cause there isn't anything left for him to look after. The spring is the most important time for vermin control, especially with wild game, and we run a line of traps along all the hedges and gateways to pick the stoats and the other ground vermin up.'

Winged predators are becoming a serious pest even in East Anglia, where magpies were virtually unknown twenty years ago. Carrion crows, jays and magpies all take a tremendous toll of eggs and young birds, and the decline in keepering has permitted them to spread, to the detriment of game and songbirds alike. Magpies in particular are extremely difficult to control and spread quickly into any vacant territory. It is an old country saying that if you kill one, then two will come to the funeral.

Foxes, too, are spreading to places where they were once unheard of, and they can be a real problem for the gamekeeper:

'I suppose I was thirty years old before I ever saw a fox. There weren't any foxes about here then, but there are now. I think it was when they did away with the gin trap that the foxes started to increase. Before that the old rabbit warreners where I came from, they each used to run six or seven dozen traps and they kept the foxes down.'

Jim has no compunction about killing foxes. The estate is on the very fringe of hunting country, and he reckons the hounds only catch a fox once in a while. The old deer park in particular provides wonderful sanctuary for the foxes, for amongst the ancient oaks, some of them up to nine hundred years old, there are countless hollow crowns and hiding places in which a vixen can rear her litter. However, like every other sensible gamekeeper, Jim has modified his view towards birds of prey. In the bad old days he used to shoot them regularly on the rearing field:

'When I first started keepering I shot seven pairs of sparrowhawks in one year. They used to come to the rearing field when we had the coops out to rear under broodies. A sparrowhawk would come to the same coop every time until she'd cleaned it out. A kestrel would hover for a start, then slip straight in and whip one and be gone. But no matter how many we used to shoot, there were still always plenty in those days. You didn't make a hole in them.'

Now, of course, sparrowhawks and kestrels are fully protected by law, and are rapidly recovering from the precarious situation which they faced when persistent pesticides had all but destroyed them. Today they are welcomed on Jim Cracknell's beat: 'There's three pairs of sparrowhawks returned here in the last five years, and I often see one about the place.'

Rough shooting provides a strong incentive for conservation

Jim believes that the key to effective vermin control is for a keeper to use his ears, his eyes and his feet. 'Watch your little birds. You learn a lot from them, and if there's anything wrong they'll tell you. If you've got an old stoat or an old cat a-prowling along a hedge, they'll tell you where he is. If there's an old hawk swing in then they'll all holler and when you hear them then you look out, 'cause you know there's something a-coming.'

'The keeper's job is to walk. These youngsters on these estates, the first thing they want is a Land-Rover, but you don't see anything if you ride. You have to walk if you want to learn anything, then if you do you'll pick everything up, you'll know every field and every bush. 'Sometimes when I go along the road I hear them pass remarks at me "What! are you standing looking over that gate with nothing to do?" Well, if you stand looking over that gate and you're using your ears and your eyes then you'll learn a lot.'

Food is the third requirement of wild game after habitat and freedom from predation. Jim and the two other keepers on the estate make sure there is plenty of food for the pheasants and partridges, especially during the winter months:

'As soon as the stubbles are up, at the end of September or the beginning of October, then we start to feed, and we feed on wheat. We've got maize as well growing on the estate as a game cover crop, and I think it's a good crop, especially for holding the partridges. If you're going to grow a cover crop, you might as well grow something that's going to provide food as well, and that's what I like about maize. It will keep feeding the birds right through the winter. 'Of course, years ago we didn't need the cover crops because all the farmers were running big herds of cows and there was kale everywhere, kale and grass. But as soon as they did away with the cows, then all the kale went.'

It would be wrong to suggest that Jim Cracknell keepers a completely wild bird shoot.

He is the first to admit that he is only just starting and like most other keepers, he rears and releases game, both pheasants and partridges, although far fewer birds are reared on the estate now than was once the case. The releasing is confined to certain parts of the shoot, and the hand-reared birds are easily recognisable from their wild counterparts. Not only are the wild pheasants much smaller, but they fly faster and are far more wary. Drive over a hill and you will soon spot the difference between a wild bird and a hand-reared one – the reared bird will eye your vehicle warily and walk cautiously away as you approach, but a wild pheasant will leg it for the nearest cover at high speed as soon as you heave into sight. Then it will head along a hedge or ditch for maybe a quarter of a mile before finally it reckons that the coast is clear enough for it to start feeding again.

When it comes to rearing partridges Helmingham has a natural advantage in that there is a ready supply of insect food for the young chicks in the form of ants' eggs.

'The old park is alive with ants' nests. There's ant hills about every yard or so, and you can get a whole sack of ants' eggs there in an hour. I shake the eggs out into a bag and take them home for the young partridges, because it gives them such a good start. You can see the little chicks start to scratch themselves and roll over as the ants get on them, and then they'll start to feed. I reckon that I can rear English partridges at ninety-seven or ninety-eight per cent on ants' eggs, but you've got to use your head, because you want to encourage them to take other food as well. It's important not to give them so many eggs that they look for them all the while, and I think a couple of feeds on ordinary partridge food followed by a feed of ants' eggs is about right.'

There are not many parts of East Anglia where old permanent pastures still exist

Just as the old-style keeper uses his initiative when it comes to feeding his birds, so he employs his own remedies when it comes to dealing with their diseases and ailments. In the old days, when pheasants were reared under broodies, there were no readily available patent medicines, and parasitic infestations could pose a serious threat to the survival of young birds. The biggest problem was gapes, a disease caused by a parasitic roundworm which infests the windpipe of game birds and poultry. If a large infestation of worms builds up, then the host bird may be asphyxiated, and in some outbreaks heavy losses may occur. Jim used to have his own secret formula for dealing with gapes, a liquid which he mixed up and put into a bottle with a perforated top. A couple of shakes of the bottle were added to each feed and then mixed in thoroughly.

'You gave the feed to them wet, usually last thing at night before closing up the coops. Then you could hear them all coughing up the worms. Sometimes they were full of worms, and I would pick up a pheasant, take a thin strand of wire and then draw the worms out of its windpipe. I once took eighteen out of one bird.'

Jim Cracknell follows a family keepering tradition. He reckons that the first thing he must have set eyes on as a youngster was a gun standing in the corner of the parlour, for both his uncle and his grandfather were keepers – indeed, his grandfather worked most of his life at Bruisyard, where Jim himself started. In 1989 Jim received a CLA long service medal at the Game Fair, which he regularly attends; after a lifetime in the job, he believes he knows the qualities of a good gamekeeper.

'A good keeper isn't made, he's born. He's got to be someone who is really keen and willing, and who doesn't look at his watch. He must love wildlife, a dog and a gun.

'I once got some good advice from an old keeper at the time when I was moving from one estate to another. He said "Jimmy boy, you're going to see a lot of fresh faces. Shut your mouth, keep your eyes and ears open, and you'll learn." Well, he was right. You can go around a farm and the old boys will tell you that you should be a-doing this or that. Just keep your mouth shut and let them tell you. Perhaps you'll know it all, but let them tell you anyway, because one day they're going to tell you something that you *don't* know.'

Jim maintains that if he had his life over again, then he wouldn't change a thing. But of course he has had the good fortune to work on a traditional estate where the old-fashioned qualities of keepering are appreciated and where the countryside is looked after and valued for its own sake rather than having the last pound's worth of profit wrung from it. The cynic might argue that it is all very well for such a place to turn its back on the more commercial forms of shooting in favour of the dilettantish pursuit of wild game. He might say that not everyone can afford to do that, just as not every shoot can afford to maintain the same number of gamekeepers today as it did thirty years ago.

But the principles which apply to the big estate apply just as well to the farm shoot which employs the services of a part-time gamekeeper, or to the small rough shoot upon which the vast majority of shooting enthusiasts in Britain rely for their recreation. They are the principles upon which the sport of shooting is based: the taking of an annual harvest of game from the countryside, a harvest which can be sustained year after year without damaging or endangering either the future prosperity of the game or the land from which it comes; a love of the countryside and respect for the plants and animals which inhabit it, coupled with the absorbing excitement which every hunting sport brings; and the fellowship and companionship which come from sharing an outdoor recreation with like-minded friends. To these the roughshooter will add the enormous pleasure which derives from working his own gundog and the thrill of being able to use his wits and his own hunting skills to bring the quarry into his possession.

Whether he has taken part in a driven shoot on a great estate or dogged a cock pheasant out of a blackberry bush on the farm next door, at the end of the day the true sportsman will be able to picture most, if not all of his shots, and to recall the sights and sounds of the countryside in which they were taken. It is the quality and variety of the bag which is important; the size is of little consequence, as any true sportsman will confirm.

The tremendous growth in interest in game shooting that has undoubtedly occurred over the past decade is to be welcomed. It has brought jobs and prosperity to a traditional sector of the rural economy, and it has provided shooting opportunity to many who would never otherwise have enjoyed it. But the development of game shooting has also brought its dark side, of which excessive bags are but one manifestation. Nevertheless, shoot management which is sympathetic to the conservation of the countryside, and a return to the traditional ways of keepering which encourage wild game, together provide a way forward. Let he who wishes merely to shoot at large numbers of airborne targets turn his attention to clay pigeon shooting. He does not need the services of a countryman and gamekeeper the like of Jim Cracknell, and neither does he deserve them.

SILVER ON THE BEACH

Working a twenty-five yard seine net along a sandy beach in the dead of night is something which involves as much skill, dedication – and exhilaration – as fishing the grandest northern river with a fly.

Ted Eales, former warden at Blakeney Point

Late on an August night the waves grate gently against a shingled shore. The North Sea lies quiet in the starlight and only a slight swell slaps against the steep-sided shingle ridge which juts eastward from the low hills of the north Norfolk coast.

Behind the shingle lies the ghostly bulk of the marram hills, soft and brooding, wafting a scent of coarse grass and warm sand onto the mild night air. Along the tideline is a jumble of jetsam. Driftwood, fish boxes ditched by a passing trawler, tattered twists of braided hawser as thick as a man's wrist, thrown overboard from a gas rig. And seaweed, drying, decaying, reeking.

A hundred yards offshore comes a splash, sounding above the growling of the surf. Then another, and then a third. The water breaks about the jumping fish, incandescent for a moment before subsiding once again into its dark slumber. The trout are running off Cley shingle bank.

Cley bank runs for some three miles between the mainland and Blakeney Point, almost parallel to the coast from which it is separated by the broad tidal waters and mudflats of Blakeney harbour. Once, centuries ago, Cley itself was a port of substance from which medieval merchants exported woollen cloth to the Low Countries. That was before the sea got to work, inexorably shifting countless tons of silt, sand and shingle, blocking the mouth of the pretty River Glaven, dividing sea from seaport with a belt of saltmarsh, and finally throwing up a storm bank of gravel and flint cobbles raised from the bed of the North Sea where they had been dumped aeons ago by the departing glaciers.

It is a quiet coast, far from the candy floss and seaside bustle of Cromer or Sheringham, and though Blakeney itself is a honeypot for visiting tourists, relatively few of them venture along the shingle bank to Blakeney Point. They are prepared to leave the lonely, wind-whipped marrams to the wheeling terns, the seals and the winter wildfowl. They leave it also to the fish which teem in the shallow coastal waters: flatfish like plaice, sole, flounder and dabs; also mackerel, mullet and, during the warm summer nights, the silvery sea trout.

Generations of longshoremen from the coastal villages have set their nets for sea trout, and among them is Ted Eales, former warden at Blakeney Point's National Trust reserve. His face wrinkled and weatherbeaten from exposure to countless North Sea storms, the backs of his hands gnarled and lumpy from rowing across Blakeney harbour at too tender an age, Ted is both a fisherman, a wildfowler and a born naturalist. As much at home with a net or a pair of binoculars as he stumped barefoot in his rolled-up canvas trousers through the marram hills, he was also deadly with a shotgun at evening flight – it was he who taught me the skills of coastal wildfowling. Ted is now retired from his duties of looking after Blakeney's world famous tern colonies, but in his younger days he fished with the best of them.

'"Drawing the shore", we used to call it. You start drawing the shore when the weather's fine, because you need a calm sea to work your net. You need to fish at night so that the trout don't see you.'

And working a twenty-five yard seine net in the dead of night is something which involves just as much skill, dedication – and exhilaration – as fishing the grandest northern river with a fly.

Crunch, crunch, crunch . . . your footsteps are deadened by the night as you top the shingle bank from the marrams and head down to where the tide is ebbing from each sandy runnel along the beach. A thin sliver of moon comes up over the horizon, but it is not the moonlight which scatters the waves into a myriad twinkling diamonds as you wade out into the water. The sea is alive with phosphorescence. Countless millions of little creatures which glow and sparkle green, white and blue with each ripple of surf. Run your hand through the tide's edge and you will see the outline of your palm and fingers picked out in a luminous underwater display. The same goes for your net which shimmers as it moves through the water.

The fishing gear to use is simplicity itself: 'You need a good bulgy net, ninety measures deep, mackerel scale, and twenty-five yards long. You'll have corks along the top line and leads along the bottom, with a good pole at each end', explains Ted.

Holding fast to the far end of the net, one man walks out into the water, going as deep as he can until he is right up to his neck in the sea. Meanwhile his partner, hanging back a few yards, walks along the tide's edge. With the net bowed between them, they draw the shore together, working out the runnels where the fishes gather, the inside man doing his best to disturb any trout which might be about, trying to drive them into the net.

It is hard work in the water, hauling twenty-five yards of sluggish, heavy net by hand, and for maybe a quarter of a mile you both walk in silence, just the sucking of the waves against the shingle breaking the night's velvet quiet. And though it is August, the North Sea is cold against your body, numbing limbs and chilling fingers. Just an old pair of jeans, a jersey and plimsolls do little to keep out the chill, and you start kicking yourself that you turned down the offer of that wet suit . . .

Then all of a sudden your reverie is interrupted. Your partner calls out 'Come in boy! Come in quick!'

You look to your left and see two darting torpedoes of phosphorescence beneath the waves, each trailing a glow of light in its wake. One hits the net, then the other. You feel the tug as two trout wrestle with the meshes and at once the whole net lights up with an electric glow. Stumbling, splashing, you draw the fishing gear up towards the beach, keeping that bottom pole hard against the sand, hoping against hope that the fish will neither slip beneath it nor leap over the top and away to freedom.

But no, you are lucky. Slithering and slapping in the tangled meshes are two fine sea trout, slab-sided and silver in the moonlight. Cold limbs and aching muscles are forgotten in a moment of elation as the two fish, each of them four or five pounds at a rough guess, are put into a canvas side bag and the net is then prepared once more for the sea.

Nobody knows from whence come the migratory sea trout which run the north Norfolk coast. But each year they would arrive early in the summer, which is when the longshoremen would start to fish.

'Early in May you very often have good catches, but the water's cold that time of year', says Ted Eales. 'The trout don't come in to feed, they come in to wash the lice off. They get lousy, you see, so they lie in the troughs of the little breakers and rub against the sand.'

Ted's best fish weighed fourteen pounds, but the most memorable night was that on which he, my father and I drew the shore down the Cley bank and in just a few hours' work netted seventy-two trout.

'That were exceptional, of course. He was lucky, your dad. We just casually went out and picked it right – there just happened to be a lot of fish in.'

We had been spending a few days up at Morston and it had been a fine, warm evening, the dying embers of the day glowing late in the clear western sky. High water was expected at around eleven o'clock at night and, shortly after dark, Ted got the fishing gear together by the light of a gas lamp which hung in the black weatherboarded shed behind the old lifeboat house on Blakeney Point. Conditions for fishing seemed just about right, a calm, warm sea and a rising tide, and if the fish were running then there was every prospect of a useful haul. Just how useful we hardly dared imagine. We couldn't put a foot wrong for most of the night. Ted, in command of the operation, gave me the task of wading up to my neck with the furthest end of the net, and each time we crossed one of those sandy gutters it seemed that the water was alive with fish, arrowing through the water and tugging at the net. Struggling breathlessly through the water, I would drag it up onto the beach with as much strength as I could muster, the silver trout slithering and wriggling under the stars as Ted deftly freed them from the meshes. No sooner had we emptied the net of one catch than it was back into the water again for another try.

For weeks afterwards we feasted on sea trout, first fresh, then out of the freezer. And the hotels and smart restaurants along the coast had sea trout on the menu for days afterwards.

That was at the time when, as a lad, I used to spend my summers up at Blakeney, hunting for rabbits in the long evenings with an old .22 bolt action rifle, going barefoot across a carpet of short-cropped turf and purple sea lavender. The place was alive with rabbits, and hares too. These were the subject of an annual hare shoot, held each year towards the end of February. It was quite an occasion, the Blakeney hare shoot, bringing

RIGHT
The marram hills – lonely and windswept

together a mixed bunch of roughshooters and wildfowlers, an assortment of weaponry in different stages of disrepair, a bevy of unruly beaters and a whole pack of dogs. There were springer spaniels, both large and small, wiry and barrel-shaped, portly golden retrievers, hounds of ancestry unknown and probably best left undiscovered, and a big black labrador with thick-set jaws and legs like tree trunks which would slurp and lap for a minute or more from a saltwater pool, then raise its tail and squirt the whole lot out of its backside with the power of a fire hose. Men stood behind that animal at their peril.

At a given signal, the posse, by now lined up across the marrams, would set off westwards towards the far end of Blakeney Point. Before long the hares started dodging through the dunes, breaking out along the shingle ridges and down to the beach. But surrounded on three sides by sea, they were forced ultimately to run the gauntlet of the guns. We never shot more than a fraction of what we saw, but it was exciting sport and it gave the dogs plenty of exercise.

At low water there was another form of fishing on the great sandflats which stretch from the high shingle ridges to the tideline. Stranded amongst the little pools left by the departing tide were dabs, little flatfish which are delicious to eat when fried in butter at tea time. Butt-pricking, it was called, the process of spearing these little dabs with a four- foot stick with a skewer affixed to the end. Trousers rolled about our knees and barefoot in the warm afternoon sunshine we walked amongst the sandy pools, eyes down, watching intently for the telltale outline of a dab. A really ace butt-pricker can feel the fish in the sand with his toes. But be careful as you strike, for that skewer is sharp, and well able to make a nasty wound in your foot.

There is a fine art in spearing a dab and lifting it cleanly out of the water, but a good afternoon's butt-pricking would often yield more than enough to provide the family with a tasty meal in the evening. Especially so if half a dozen dabs are augmented with a good sized bunch of samphire, the bright green spikes known otherwise as glasswort, which grows all around the edge of the saltings.

Ted Eales started fishing at the age of twelve. His father had been in the coastguard, stationed in Essex, and as a youngster Ted lived on the north side of the Blackwater at Goldhanger, in one of a pair of red brick coastguard cottages. Even today you can just make out the whitened brickwork around the doorway, which Ted's father had to limewash once a year, back in the early 1920s. Many years later, Ted himself was to play an active role in the coastguard service, and the certificate which he was awarded for his part in one particular life-saving rescue is a treasured possession.

'After the coastguard, my father got the job up at Blakeney. That would have been when I was about five. We did a lot of fishing when I was a lad. Years ago, you'd get a lot of different fish. Mullet, we got, and nice little flatfish – plaice, dabs, flounders. And turbot, I'd love to get them, about the size of a dinner plate.'

But the most exciting fishing was for trout. They were caught either by drawing the shore at night or by fishing from a dinghy with a 120 yard net during the daylight hours. After rowing out to the fishing ground, the netsman pulled his boat round in a big semicircle, paying out the net as he went. With luck he'd pick up a few trout or mullet, but it took fine judgement to haul the net at just the right time to prevent the lively fish from jumping over the bobbing line of corks and away to sea.

Whitebait were a local delicacy, and the whitebait swarmed in silver shoals off the point and around the entrance to Blakeney harbour. A number of fishermen pursued them in season, one or two making a reasonable living at doing so. You could always tell the location of the whitebait shoals by watching the terns, which fed voraciously on the tiny fish. To see a whitebait shoal under attack from terns at the height of the nesting season is quite astonishing. The water boils as the birds plunge vertically into the sea, reappearing moments later with fish in their beaks, which they carry back to the terneries for their hungry chicks. As they return to shore their places are taken by dozens more terns, each awaiting its chance to dive upon the shoal. Meanwhile below the water the whitebait form a living ball, each fish trying to get nearer the centre to escape the predators above, as those on the outside of the mass are picked off in their hundreds.

Then there was the mackerel fishing. The longshoremen would take their boats out of Blakeney and Morston in the earliest light of a summer morning, as the stars dimmed and the first froth-flecked fingers of tide edged their way up Morston creek. Once out of the marked channel, a course was set westwards, around the grey bulk of Blakeney Point, passing the old lifeboat house to starboard, out beyond the seal banks and into the open waters of the North Sea, still pink with the reflection of breaking dawn. In the old days, the mackerel fishermen used spinners, trolling them behind the boats. The fishermen who knew where to find the shoals of mackerel could make good catches – maybe three or four hundred before breakfast time.

Later on, they changed to the Norwegian system of fishing, using feathered flies. With seven or eight flies on a line, you first find the mackerel, then cut the engine and let your boat drift, dabbing the line up and down to attract the fish. There is sufficient movement in

The old lifeboat house and (*inset*) the wreck of the 'Yankee clipper'

the brightly coloured flies as they dart up and down through the water to bring the fish swarming around each line. But of course the trick is knowing where to find the mackerel. That's where modern technology comes into play, for these days the more canny mackerel fishermen arm themselves with echo sounders.

There are still mackerel caught off Blakeney, but in recent years the longshoremen have met with increasing competition from another highly efficient species of fisherman. Blakeney has long been noted for its seal colony, and though the local people always tolerated the seals, matters were never allowed to get out of hand, as Ted explained.

'When the seals got too numerous the Ministry of Agriculture and Fisheries used to give us ten bob a nose to kill them. There were three or four men getting a living from the flatfish in Blakeney harbour in those days, and one year the fishing got so bad that everyone complained to the ministry. They had so many complaints that they got hold of a couple of us locals and told us that they wanted at least half a dozen seals.

'We took a couple of rifles out with us in a boat and the ministry men came with us. I suppose we got eight or nine seals, which this scientist fellow cut the stomachs out of and took back with him to Cambridge. They checked the seals' insides to see what they were feeding on, and found that this lot of seals were eating whelks.

'They had digested every part of these whelks, shells and all. The whole lot, except for the very points of the shells.'

Blakeney's flatfish men may have been surprised at the findings of the Fisheries Department's scientists, but the Wells fishermen just a few miles along the coast viewed the matter with considerably more interest and not a little concern, for they made their living catching whelks. At one time there was a whelk fishery at Blakeney, but now the whelks are far out to sea, and the Wells men might have to go fifteen or twenty miles offshore to find the whelk beds.

Whelks were only one of the shellfish which the local longshoremen harvested. Years ago there were oyster layings, and of course there were always mussels – big blue ones with a flavour which is hard to match when they are boiled up with fresh onions, butter, parsley and a dash of white wine. These days fewer mussels are landed locally because of strict regulations surrounding the size of the shellfish which can be taken. And along the coast at Stiffkey were the famous 'Stewkey blues', great fat cockles with shells the delicate colour of pale slate and a rich succulent flavour. The cockle beds are far out on the sandflats which stretch from Blakeney Point to the distant clumps of Scots pine which mark the beginning of Lord Leicester's Holkham estate.

The fishing along this stretch of coast these days is now but a shadow of its former self. Ironically it is the seals which today provide valuable income to the local boatmen. Popular interest in the seal colony has never been greater, especially since the terrible epidemic which wiped out half of the east coast's breeding population of common seals in the summer of 1988. Instead of taking parties of visitors to the point, the pleasure boats now run a round trip to visit the seals. Basking like fat, grey dogs on the sandbanks at the harbour's mouth, the seals gaze with curiosity at the visitors and the tourists stare back. While at sea the seals are supremely confident, and will swim to within a few feet of a passing boat or bob about just a stone's throw from the beach as you walk to the water's edge; but come too close to them when they are ashore and they scuttle into the water in a wild, ungainly and faintly ludicrous panic.

One day, hopefully, the seal colony will recover from its population crash, but meanwhile the bones lie bleaching along the high water mark, sad and pathetic remains of those animals which succumbed to disease and perished. Perhaps the plague was a lesson to us, for nature has a way of controlling herself. It is now many years since the seals were protected and the modest annual cull was abandoned. Could it be that the consequent growth in the seal numbers had something to do with the way in which the disease, once it caught hold, was allowed to spread rapidly and unchecked?

'Conservation, they call it,' sighs Ted Eales. Like all his generation of countrymen, he was brought up to appreciate that the natural order of things is a matter of checks and balances, and that human management – interference if you like – may control one species in order to benefit another. Control, mark you, not eliminate. The good wildlife warden is like the good gamekeeper, whose twin tasks are maintaining the optimum habitat for game and controlling those species which most seriously prey upon it. It was rare to find a hedgehog on the point when Ted was there, for Mrs Tiggywinkle is no friend to ground-nesting birds. And so the terns thrived and the terneries ultimately became amongst the most noted in the world.

Ted loved his terns with a rare passion, and remains a formidable authority on them. His knowledge, however, was not gained from the study of dry, technical scientific tomes but characteristically from direct observation in the field, as befitted a true countryman. Indeed, he delighted in criticising the bird books. For years they copied one another and perpetuated what to Ted was a glaring error, by colouring the legs of the little tern chick yellow instead of a flesh tint. It was the cause of much ribald mirth, and he was in no hurry to help the experts correct their misapprehension. If the 'bush bashers' wanted to know anything, then as far as Ted was concerned they could jolly well row over to the point and ask him. A 'bush basher' was Ted's term for a bird watcher. It was derived from the predeliction of some of the more eager members of the twitching fraternity of beating the bushes along the coast in an effort to dislodge some wretched newly arrived migrant from its slumbers that they might tick it off their list. Ted had little time for twitchers.

Neither had he much patience for those visitors who strayed amongst his precious terneries. He devised a method of marking out the nesting areas with strands of binder twine: while the visitors kept to their own side of the string all was well and the terns remained on their nests, but the moment a single person put a foot over the fragile boundary, vengeance was swift. In a moment the terns would launch a dive-bombing attack on the intruder, and in some cases could do real damage with their sharp beaks.

When he retired from the National Trust, Ted maintained his involvement with wildlife, presenting Anglia Television's 'Countryman' programme, and becoming a familiar and much loved character on the television screens of eastern England. Now in his seventies, he has moved away from the house he had built at Morston – constructed for a seafaring man to ship's specifications with living quarters aloft and cabins below decks – and today he lives with his wife Betty in the quiet north Norfolk countryside.

However, it is hard to think of him in anything other than that old woolly hat, a jersey and canvas trousers, plimsolls on his feet and a net slung over his shoulder. Or perhaps, on a winter's eve, crouched amongst the sueda bushes along the shore in waders and tattered oilskin jacket, waiting for the wigeon to come in over some bleak shingle ridge as the sky dims across Blakeney harbour and the first flecks of snow spiral out of the grey gloom.

GUNNERS OF THE TIDE

Using techniques and equipment essentially unchanged since the early nineteenth century, the punt gunner stalks the ever changing mudflats and watery wastes where the tides ebb and flow, trusting to his skill in order to get his shallow craft within range of a pack of wary ducks.

Punt gunning on the Essex coast

In the last hour before dawn on a midwinter's morning, a car draws up to the gate which leads from the bottom of a quiet lane down to a sea wall enclosing a narrow, winding creek. There, amongst the small collection of fishing smacks and overwintering sailing cruisers, their masts leaning at drunken angles as they lie at rest on the mud, their dark forms barely visible through the grey gloom, the last of the tide is ebbing away. The two men who climb out of the vehicle set to work with a sense of urgency. By torchlight they don thigh waders, white jerseys and pale grey smocks which make them appear almost ghostly against the black December oaks, whose bare twigs drip moisture onto the dank grass beneath.

They ferry a collection of gear from the car in the direction of the creek: oars, paddles and poles, a short mast with a small sail furled around it, bags, boxes and a couple of guns slung in canvas slips about their shoulders. They hurry along the short footpath which leads to the creek and dump their gear in a heap on the top of the sea wall, then, returning to the car, they set about unlashing a large grey gun barrel from the roof rack. The weapon is eight feet long and about an inch and a half in diameter, and the two men bend visibly under its weight as it, too, is manhandled down to the creek.

Lying on the mud, its cockpit sheathed in a canvas cover, is the long, lean shape of a boat, a gunning punt, to which our two wildfowlers transport their equipment. Working with a will, they lug their gear down the sea wall and over the sticky mud, the sucking of their waders in the thick ooze and the hoarse pant of their laboured breathing echoing about the creek as they do so. The big gun is heaved on board and laid along the low foredeck, the stem and stern lines are released and then, with a Herculean effort, the two men heave the punt across the mud, pushing and shoving it towards the last few inches of water that are now running out of the bottom of the creek. The punt starts to slide and slither over the mud, and then slips quietly into the water.

Immediately it is transformed from an ungainly, lumbering and reluctant hulk to a thing of beauty, low, sleek and almost sinister; a slim, grey, rakish shark of a boat amongst the tubby fishing vessels which lean over it. The two wildfowlers climb aboard and pole quietly downstream. The haste, the lung-bursting effort and pounding heartbeats are suddenly forgotten as the punt glides silently towards the greying eastern horizon, and the only sound to be heard is that of a startled redshank, hurriedly departing the tideline as the grey wraith ghosts past, just a few feet away. In a couple of minutes the punt's pale colouring merges with the mirror grey of the water and the misty morning sky, and the boat and its two occupants disappear from view.

For three hundred years or more, men have pursued wildfowl with large bore fowling pieces attached to boats of various sorts, and in those areas where large numbers of ducks and geese have regularly overwintered – coastal estuaries and flooded fens – local traditions of punt gunning grew up. At one time, all the gunners of those parts were professionals, local men who shot fowl for the market to provide themselves and their families with a living. But in the opening years of the nineteenth century a new breed of amateur punt gunners was born, men who recognised the excitement, adventure and the enormous challenge of wildfowl shooting afloat, and who developed punt gunning into a sport with its own code of ethics.

Amateurs and professionals punted side by side, sharing – sometimes uneasily – the same berths and launching places, the visiting gentleman gunner frequently employing a

local puntsman rather as a salmon fisherman might engage a ghillie. But slowly professional punt gunning declined. Many of the great inland fens and marshes were drained to provide new farmland, sweeping away the old way of life of the fowlers and fishermen. Inland punt gunning was effectively dead by the nineteen-fifties, although its spirit lived on in the hands of one or two old-timers for another twenty years. On the coast too, the new postwar prosperity finally put paid to the era of the professional gunner as the longshoreman found new, more attractive and more comfortable ways of making a living. And so the amateur punt gunner found himself alone on the traditional estuarine fowling grounds, his sport, his techniques, even his equipment essentially unchanged from the early years of the nineteenth century.

While the shorebound wildfowler does his best to get under a flight line in the morning or evening when the ducks and geese are on the move, or waits for the tide to push birds over him, the punt gunner actively goes in search of wildfowl far out in a wilderness of mud and water. His is a stalking sport, the essence of which is to endeavour to creep to within around seventy yards of a flock of wildfowl on the tide's edge and then to fire a charge of heavy shot into the midst of them in an attempt to bag a number of birds at a single discharge. Punting is far removed from wildfowling with a shoulder gun, indeed it is closer if anything to stalking wild red deer on the hill than to flight shooting on the salt marsh, though at least the hill stalker is able to make use of the natural ground cover around him in order to engineer his approach and then get close enough to the deer to make his shot. The punt gunner has no such cover to hide him. His stalking grounds are the ever-changing mudflats and watery wastes where the tides ebb and flow. He must use the wind, the light and the current to aid his approach, and trust to his skill in order to get his low, shallow craft within range of a pack of wary ducks.

In doing so the punt gunner is at the mercy of the elements, and especially the wind. Whereas the flight shooter prays for gales to keep the birds on the move and low enough to shoot at as they fly over him, the punt gunner needs calm weather or at most a light breeze. Anything more will make his small craft impossible to manoeuvre, and even a moderately choppy sea can swamp a gun punt which has no more than a few inches of freeboard. In that respect the old-fashioned open-decked punts of the professional gunners were regular death traps. Lacking either foredeck, side decks or coaming to keep out the sea, the open punt was a dangerous craft to navigate in any but the most enclosed waters. The traditional open Essex punt was sometimes referred to as a floating coffin, and only half in jest, for even a sheltered estuary can blow up rough at a frightening speed.

While almost all the professional gunners worked their punts single-handed, most punt gunners today operate the slightly larger double-handed craft. A double punt, being longer and wider in the beam, will withstand considerably rougher weather than a single, but the main reason for punting with a partner is for the companionship, for someone with whom to share the hard work of rowing or poling, the intense excitement of the stalk or simply the breathtaking beauty of the estuary. A full day on the water can be a long time to spend on your own.

A gun punt is a small and fragile craft in which to put to sea, and tradition dictates that it is powered by the muscles of its occupants and by the natural forces of wind and tide alone. In fact the 1981 Wildlife and Countryside Act enshrined this point in law when it prohibited the use of any mechanically propelled craft in the immediate pursuit of wild birds. Motorised gun punts were not unknown in the past, and indeed elaborate plans were published for the construction and use of such vessels. However, punt gunning today relies as it always has done on the use of oars, paddles, poles and sails; and since the draught of a punt should be no more than four inches or so – any more and it would constantly be running aground – centreboards or fixed keels are ruled out. This means that a punt under sail is virtually restricted to running and reaching.

Gunning punts respond well under sail, and in Norfolk the traditional design of the wildfowling punt was many years ago adapted by the sailing fraternity into a thoroughbred racing craft. There are few Norfolk punts still sailing today, but those which remain are boats of great beauty and awesome speed, whose traditional lines betray their origin in the 'fowling craft of Breydon Water and the broads. Because sailing a working gun punt only becomes profitable when the wind speed is close to force four, or at least ten knots – marginal conditions in which to set to sea – the small spritsail which she carries as part of her equipment is only infrequently used. But what a joy when it is, especially if you are homeward bound after a long trip and weary of rowing and poling.

His means of propulsion being limited, the punt gunner has to work with the tide, punting downriver on the ebb and stalking back on the flood, so he may well be afloat for eight hours or more, travelling many miles before returning to his mooring. On any particular estuary there will be only three or four days each fortnightly cycle in which the tides permit an early morning departure and a return to base before the end of a short winter's day. During this time the best chance of a shot will be around the hour of low water, when the wildfowl gather on the furthest muds to feed, and as the tide starts to make. Then, in the first two or three hours of the flood, wildfowl will bunch around the advancing tideline and the puntsman will have a chance of creeping quietly up to them, working his way with stealth and caution over the shallows until he is within shot. On a falling tide his job is infinitely harder, for as he makes his way slowly towards the ducks bunched enticingly ahead of him on a drying mudbank, he stands every chance of running aground if he is not careful to plan his approach to follow deep water.

Having spent half an hour or more working with infinite care and in dead silence up to a pack of wigeon dabbling in the shallows, stopping each time it seems as though they might detect the danger nearby, then making the final adjustments to the big gun, there are few things more frustrating than to run aground a hundred yards away from the nearest bird. Ahead is the whistling and splashing of twenty or more wigeon, quite oblivious to your presence yet too far away to shoot at, and here are you stuck fast on the mud, with the tide running away all around you. There is nothing for it but for you and your partner to get out of the punt, waving the wigeon goodbye in the process, and to push her off into deeper water before you find yourselves high and dry for the next six hours.

At the start of a punting expedition, slipping downstream on the ebb with the yellow glow of sunrise filtering through the grey morning mist and reflecting off the water, you feel a thousand miles away from the rest of humanity, totally absorbed in the business of propelling and manoeuvring the punt, navigating her towards some distant spot where the wigeon might gather and keeping a constant eye ahead for the first sign of wildfowl activity. Always the field glasses are at the ready, probing into the morning mist, checking out every bird along the shoreline, focussing upon each distant silhouette afloat on the tide. Probably more than any other wildfowler, the punt gunner has to be an accomplished

Jonathan Yule 90

naturalist, for he is likely to see many different species of wildfowl and waders during the course of the day, each of which he must be able to identify, but without disturbing any of them in the process. It is no earthly good confirming that a pack of likely looking birds are in fact legitimate quarry only when they take to the air in flight and disappear over the horizon.

Down on the wide waters of the lower estuary are many birds of which the shore shooter gets at the most only a distant glimpse. Big flocks of goldeneye ride out the tide, the brilliant plumage of the drakes standing out black and white in the morning light. Cormorants rest on a shingle bank, their wings held open like so much black washing hanging out to dry. Mergansers patrol in pairs, their long saw-toothed bills and slender necks making a graceful picture on the water. Afloat on the estuaries of Essex I have sometimes come across a party of long tailed ducks, a protected species which spends most of its time at sea and is rarely seen close to the shoreline, their jovial-looking chocolate brown and white faces contrasting with the elegance of their delicate tails. Other wildlife is to be seen out on the river. Before the crash in the seal population in the North Sea I frequently had a common seal follow my punt downstream, its head popping up like that of a labrador just a few feet astern of where I was sitting, then disappearing again beneath the water with a slight plop.

On the downstream journey there may be time to try a practice stalk in order to check the elevation of the gun and ensure that both gunner and puntsman know exactly what will be required of them when the time comes to set to fowl in deadly earnest. It is fun to push up to a party of brent geese, protected now but once one of the main quarry species pursued by the punt gunner. Slowly you move in on a pack feeding along the shoreline. When you judge them to be in range you adjust the elevating rest on which the gun barrel sits, so that the muzzle is trained on the feet of the nearest goose. Then you back off, leaving them unaware that they were ever just seventy yards from mortal danger.

It frequently comes as a surprise to those who see a punt gun for the first time to learn that the effective range of such a weapon is only twice that of an ordinary twelve bore shoulder gun. Ought not something which looks like a piece of naval ordnance to have a range of hundreds of yards, they ask. And so it would, were it to be loaded like a naval gun with a solid projectile. But a punt gun, like any other shot gun, is essentially a short range weapon and dependent for its effectiveness upon its ability to deliver an even pattern of heavy shot over relatively modest distances. The gunner who tries to shoot ducks at excessive ranges soon learns that although such tactics may once in a while bring off a lucky kill, more often they will result in wounded quarry, with all the anxiety entailed in collecting and despatching it.

In fact the punt gunner, if he judges his range correctly before firing, should rarely have wounded birds to deal with. The heavy shot which a punt gun handles, normally size 1 or BB, retains enormous striking energy over seventy to eighty yards when thrown by three ounces or so of coarse grain black powder. A single pellet is quite sufficient to kill a duck outright in most circumstances, and if by chance it does not, then the gunner carries a regular twelve bore shoulder gun in the punt with which he can quickly deal with the wounded. Since punt gunning is conducted over bare, open mudflats and tidal creeks, there is virtually no cover in which a wounded duck can hide, so it is not especially difficult to recover even a lightly winged duck.

There are, however, a few rules to gathering winged birds. First of all, only the most foolhardy gunner carries a loaded shoulder gun in the punt. The normal place in which to stow the twelve bore is under the side deck in a gun rack, and if it were to get knocked by a pole or an oar, then there would be every likelihood of blowing the side out of the punt, at the very least. To be left with a large hole in one's punt and several miles of angry water to navigate before reaching safety is not recommended.

Then if a shot is made and you have to chase over the mud to collect your birds, always remember to drop the anchor and chain overboard before leaving the punt. It is surprising how quickly the tide rises around a punt which, only a few moments before, was thought to be firmly pulled up onto the mud. Believe me, it is no joke to struggle back through the ooze, having collected together the results of your shot, only to see your punt drifting rapidly away in the wind. I have only done it once, and that time I got away with two waders full of water and a severe fright. Half a minute more and the whole outfit, gun and all, would have been caught by the westerly breeze and sent on its way to Holland.

Most punt gunners endeavour to take their shots whilst the birds are grouped on the mud or around the tide's edge, because under these circumstances they offer the largest possible target area and thus make a clean kill more certain. Rarely is it possible to make a reasonable shot at ducks which are afloat on the water, for in general they are not grouped sufficiently tightly. If there is any sort of wind blowing, the birds start bobbing up and down whilst the swell sets the punt itself pitching so much that an accurate shot is extremely difficult. In any case, a large proportion of the potential target area of a swimming duck is under water. The old gunners, who would not miss a chance of any sort, would overcome this latter disadvantage by kicking the side of the punt at the crucial moment to put the birds' heads up before pulling the lanyard and letting drive. The real experts let them jump and then take a flying shot, but unless you are a pretty competent shot with a punt gun, that is the most likely way of courting a clean miss. And it is just as easy to miss with a punt gun than with any other sort of weapon.

On any punt gunning expedition the chances of a shot are likely to be few, because no gunner worth his salt is going to discharge a punt gun unless there is a reasonable bag to be made: a shot which reflects the size of his gun, the local conditions within the estuary in which he is punting and the personal standard or level of expectation which he sets himself. Frequently a trip lasting seven or eight hours will end without a shot being fired, possibly because insufficient quarry ducks were seen but more likely because the birds were in some unapproachable spot, were too wary, or had protected species in their midst. Sometimes a gunner will go out for several days before finding a shot which he judges to be worth taking.

Thus the pleasures of punting derive only in small part from the successfully executed stalk. Much more it is the beauty of the wild estuary which brings the rewards, the opportunity to be alone amongst the waders on the shoreline or to see the orange glow of a late afternoon shaft of sunlight filtering through the dank, raw overcast sky, throwing each pebble on the muddy foreshore into sharp relief and colouring the little wavelets which scud across the shallows. Perhaps on the homeward journey it is the dip of the oars into the mirror-calm surface of the river, glowing pink like so much liquid pearl, the reflections in the water as a passing skein of brent geese dip low on downward arching wings, and the cry of the redshank as the flood tide laps around the green, decaying

timbers of some old wrecked barge. And on a Sunday morning at low water, far out in the middle of the estuary on some mudbank, it is the silvery sound of bells from the waterside villages, rising and falling on the mild, clear air. No wonder punt gunning is a sport which over the years has appealed to so many artists and writers.

When it comes, however, the excitement of setting to fowl in a gunning punt is intense and quite unlike any other experience in the world of shooting sports. Perhaps a quarter of a mile away you and your partner have spotted a likely looking group of ducks through the field glasses, gathering on the edge of a mudbank which, a couple of hours after low water, is just starting to disappear beneath the flowing tide. Both gunner and puntsman check out the birds and confer. They look like nothing more than a thin dark line against the grey mud from where you are on the edge of a deep water channel. It is heavily overcast and the light is not good, but they seem as if they could well be wigeon. Certainly worth a closer look.

The gear is prepared in readiness for the possibility of a shot. Making a rough estimate of the depth of water ahead, the puntsman elects to use a setting pole. There will be no need to cross any deep channels on the approach to where the birds are sitting, so he should not find himself out of his depth halfway through the stalk. He opens one of the flaps in the coaming to enable him to work the pole over the side of the punt without being seen by the birds. Meanwhile the gunner arranges his equipment. The twelve bore is placed where it will be immediately available if necessary, the magazine – which doubles up as a rowing seat when required – is positioned close to the breech of the big gun to form a rest on which the gunner can lie, and all extraneous bags, poles and oars are stowed away to make as much room as possible. Finally the gunner places his field glasses on the floor of the punt beside him.

You both lie flat in the punt and the puntsman starts his approach. There is no problem with the light: it's flat and grey, so the punt should blend well with the water and sky astern. But there's a bit of difficulty with the wind. A nasty little breeze is coming in off the starboard bow. It keeps trying to swing the punt off line and makes the puntsman's tough job a touch harder. It is also moving the bows of the punt up and down, and the gunner makes a mental note to allow for the chop on the water should it come to a shot.

Three hundred yards now, and a peep through the glasses confirms that there are indeed wigeon ahead, about forty of them and well up on the mud. They are quite strung out along the tideline, but there seem to be one or two thicker groups at which the gunner might aim. You whisper to each other, pause for a moment, then shrink down flat into the punt. It all looks good and the birds haven't spotted anything amiss. With a click the cocking lever is drawn back and the lanyard gripped tightly.

Now there is just the quiet slap of water against the bows of the punt, the hoarse breathing of the puntsman, driving the slim craft forward with long, powerful strokes, the distant sound of ripples breaking on the shoreline and the whistle of a single cock wigeon. And two hearts pound against the floorboards of the punt.

At two hundred yards you come into unexpectedly shallow water. The puntsman struggles, for his pole is really too long to manage in what is now no more than six or seven inches of depth, but he knows that to change now to the short setting sprits would make too much noise and movement. He is committed. Then disaster strikes: he runs aground. The punt scrapes harshly on the mud and stones below, and the best efforts of the puntsman will not shift it. Muttered oaths and curses emanate from the engine room, but still the birds have not twigged your presence and there is yet hope of recovering the situation before they do. Thank heavens you are working a flood tide. It has been twenty minutes since you first spotted the ducks, and now it will probably be another five before there is sufficient water underneath the punt to float her again. You both lie still and wait.

What seems like an age later, a slight grinding noise below indicates that the tide is doing its stuff, and the puntsman tests the situation with an exploratory shove. The punt inches forward, then three or four mighty heaves and she is afloat again, and in a good depth of water. You realise that you have just come over the top of a submerged mudbank, and mark its position for the future. A hundred and fifty yards, and you agree which part of the flock to head for. Terse, whispered instructions from gunner to puntsman: 'Go for the bunch on the left, eleven o'clock'.

The bows swing round a few degrees and catch a little gust of wind. A hundred yards. Two old cocks at the edge of the flock put their heads up, and you both freeze. Will they jump now? Have they seen the punt which is bearing down upon them with such stealth? 'Please don't jump, not now!', mutters the gunner. Suffering in silence, the puntsman can only agree. The heads go down, and once again you inch forward.

It is the final stage of the approach. Seventy yards and you're in range, but much better to try and get a little closer still. Sighting down the side of the barrel, the gunner makes final checks for line and elevation, steadies the gun and gets ready to pull. They've seen you! In a flash all the heads are up, but by now it is too late for them. At sixty-five yards you fire instantly. There is a great WHOOMPH as twelve ounces of shot accelerate into space, a mighty roar which rolls and resounds around the deserted estuary, but of which you are strangely unaware, for every atom of your attention is still concentrated on the mudbank which lies ahead.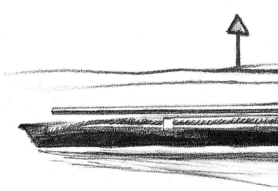

You are aware of the birds jumping through a thick white cloud of powder smoke. The shot must have been a trifle low, either that or those wigeon jumped faster than you had expected, but all is not lost, for you can see at least half a dozen birds lying on the mud and one more kicking feebly in the shallows. The puntsman pushes his craft ashore and, grabbing the twelve bore just in case, the gunner gets out. It does not take him long to collect the ducks – first the one in the water, a gorgeous cock in his plumage of black, white and dusky pink, with chestnut head and yellow forehead flash, then the others, hens mostly, and all of them fat as butter. The total bag is eight, not as many as it might have been, but a useful shot nevertheless.

It is a full forty minutes since you first spotted the fowl, and it is time for a well-earned cup of coffee. Nowhere, at this moment, are there two more satisfied and contented wild-fowlers, hunters whom chance placed within those same few wild miles of mud and water as their quarry and whose skill, teamwork and sheer effort has put that quarry within their grasp. What satisfaction those eight birds have brought, a moment which will be remembered long after their fellows have flown back beyond the Arctic Circle, a shot which has set the final physical seal of success on a tough, exacting, but deeply enjoyable day.

Of course it isn't always like that. More often there will be some factor which causes the birds to jump whilst they are still out of range. Perhaps you have to approach them out of a bright sunlit sea against which your small punt stands out like a battleship, or maybe it is just that the ducks are edgy and nervous. In this respect there is a wide difference in the behaviour of the different quarry species. Mallard, for instance, are notoriously difficult to approach, and pintail even more so. Wigeon and teal, on the other hand, generally present a better opportunity.

The most galling disaster to beset the punt gunner is a misfire. To have spent the best part of a day on the water searching for a shot, to have set to a pack of birds, brought the big gun to within range and pulled the lanyard, only to be rewarded with a damp phut, is a thoroughly demoralising experience. Even worse is a hang fire, when the phut, just loud enough to startle the birds into making good their escape, is followed by the boom of the main charge scything into a by then empty mudbank. If this should happen, then one simply has to be philosophical: there will be more duck, more chances, another day's gunning on the tide.

All true wildfowling, and from this category I deliberately exclude most – though not all – inland duck shooting, is physically demanding and has about it, at least in some measure, the spice of danger. The element of risk is a powerful attraction in some field sports, turning the pursuit of the quarry into a real challenge which in some sense shortens the odds between hunter and hunted. The covert shooter may well find the high driven pheasant a testing target, but the test is solely one of his own proficiency with a gun. It does not involve any trial of physical stamina, skill in woodcraft or venery, and neither does it entail any contest with the natural elements. This is not to suggest that covert shooting is by definition a lesser sport, merely that its pleasures are different. Wildfowling, on the other hand, has a number of challenges built into it, the challenge between a hunter and his quarry, the physical challenge which the hunter sets himself and the challenge between man and the elements. Foxhunting, another great risk sport, contains similar challenges.

Of all forms of wildfowling, punt gunning is both the most demanding and that which carries the most risk. There is always a potential danger in setting to sea in a small boat, no matter what precautions are taken, and he who does not treat the estuary with a healthy respect is a fool. Weather forecasters can always make mistakes, and even though the prediction was for nothing more than a light breeze, that is no consolation if you are several miles from home and far out in the most exposed part of the river when the squall strikes. It does not take long for a punt to fill with water under such circumstances, and it is a frightening experience to find the sea pouring across the foredeck and driving over the coaming faster than you are able to bale. As you toss helplessly adrift amongst the breaking waves, oars and paddles start to float around in the bottom of the punt, and before long the punt begins to wallow like a drowning animal. The only chance of salvation then, if there is no convenient lee shore against which you can drift, is to heave the big gun overboard, having first attached a line and buoy to it so that its position is marked. With so much dead weight removed, there is more chance of saving the punt and yourself.

Ditching the big gun is not an everyday occurrence but it does happen from time to time, and recovering it from the sea can be a dangerous task in its own right. One highly experienced Essex gunner who was obliged to drop his valuable punt gun overboard, subsequently sought to retrieve his property with the aid of a local fisherman. Reaching the spot where the gun lay, he hauled upon the stout line which he had attached to the weapon and eventually brought the breech above the waves, whereupon the fisherman grabbed the most convenient looking bit of line and pulled. The line happened to be the cocking lanyard and the gun happened to be loaded. As it turned out, the mystery of whether or not three ounces of black powder in a waterproof cartridge can survive intact at the bottom of a tidal river for twenty-four hours was never solved. When, in words laced with the choicest invective, the fellow was told the real purpose of the string upon which he was pulling, he dropped the gun in horror. Luckily no damage was done, but a discharge at that moment could at the very least have blown his small fishing boat clean out of the water.

Another danger is fog. Although one should never go punting in a dense fog, visibility can sometimes deteriorate very rapidly and without any warning whatsoever. One moment familiar landmarks can be seen on all quarters and the next they are shrouded in dense, clammy vapour. Then all thoughts of fowling are put aside and the survival instinct takes over. A good compass is an essential part of the punt gunner's equipment, and no less important is the skill with which to use it. On more than one occasion I have had to navigate home on a compass bearing, with visibility down to less than twenty-five yards, and it is in such circumstances that you quickly learn the value of a good chart.

Various noted punt gunners have commented upon the danger of getting too close to the breech end of a punt gun when firing it, something which, in the excitement of a stalk, it is all too easy for the novice gunner to do. Although the recoil of the big gun is absorbed by a breeching rope which is passed through a hole in the bows of the punt and its ends fixed to trunnions mounted on the gun itself, a punt gun can still kick like a mule, and must be treated with great respect. Sir Ralph Payne-Gallwey made the classic comment when he advocated the use of a safety strap in addition to the standard breeching rope:

> 'When you have re-arranged, as best you can, your battered features, mopped the blood from your face, and, if your eyes are not closed, picked off the floor of the punt those of your teeth that were not knocked down your throat or overboard, you will, perhaps, be ready to admit, when too late, that a safety fastening to your stanchion gun would have been an advantage.'

The scenario which Payne-Gallwey describes is by no means fanciful; in fact it happened just a few seasons back to a novice gunner of my acquaintance. Although warned to keep his face clear of the gun butt when firing, enthusiasm overcame his natural caution. Even though the breeching rope absorbed the bulk of the recoil, the discharge still knocked out most of the poor chap's front teeth, and he had to be rushed to a nearby farm from where emergency dental aid could be summoned. I believe I am right in saying that he never went out punt gunning again.

Punt gunning is an active, exciting sport which demands great physical fitness from its participants and which contains a significant element of danger. Yet notwithstanding these facts it receives more than its fair share of criticism from those who believe that punt gunners take unduly large bags of birds and cause excessive disturbance to the wildlife of the estuary in doing so.

In fact, the number of ducks shot by the few dozen active punt gunners who still ply the tide is infinitesimal when compared to the quantity killed by the 170,000 duck shooters who operate with shoulder guns. In terms of overall wildfowl population management, the effect of punt gunning is so small as to be invisible. Even when brought down to the level of the individual shooter, the contention that punt gunners are guilty of taking too many birds simply does not stand up to logical argument. For an individual gun to shoot eight or nine wild ducks at a flight pond would not be considered extraordinary, yet this represents about the average punt shot. And whereas the flight shooter will be happy if he can kill his eight ducks with twenty-five shots, the punt gunner will have used only one. In fact there are those who kill a good many more than eight wild ducks at a sitting. Heavily fed flight ponds around the east coast sometimes take well over a hundred ducks with eight or ten guns shooting at evening flight, and individual guns will occasionally kill far more than that – in fact one noted shooter recently boasted of having shot over two hundred and ninety wild ducks to his own pair of guns in a single day. Frankly, such a feat is not something about which I would care to boast.

The quantity of ducks which a team of guns at a commercial duck shoot will kill in a day makes the average punt gunner's bag look like something out of Toytown. Two or three hundred hand-reared mallard is no more than an average day at some of these establishments, while the really big pheasant shoots put even bags of this magnitude in the shade. Can it really be considered acceptable for the game shot to kill sixty pheasants to his own gun in a day's covert shooting, yet improper for the punt gunner to take eight wigeon?

Charges of disturbance are levelled against punt gunners just as they are against others who pursue wildfowl along the shoreline, but the irony is that the punt gunner's main objective is to cause as little disturbance as possible. As has been observed, his is a stalking sport, and the stalker who frightens his quarry away before he reaches it has nothing left to stalk. The quiet passage of a punt raises little alarm amongst wildfowl and waders – knot, dunlin and oystercatchers will continue feeding when a gun punt is in full view only yards away, and I have on occasions got so close to sleeping wigeon that it would have been possible, had I felt so inclined, to have reached over the coaming and picked them off the surface of the water with my hand.

If he does get to discharge his piece, the punt gunner will be lucky if he gets more than a single shot in a day. Yet judging by the number of cartridges most shoulder gunners appear to get through in the course of a season, they frequently fire rather more than that on a morning or evening flight, and the disturbance they cause is consequently greater.

Punt gunning is by far the hardest way of winning wildfowl. When you take into account the amount of time which is spent not only on the water in active pursuit of game, but also on dry land preparing and transporting the necessary equipment and, out of season, repairing and maintaining it, you can quite easily see that punt gunning is a sport which requires no less than total commitment. Perhaps that is why it is so fascinating.

PTARMIGAN HILLS

Ptarmigan shooting in the Highlands is quite unlike any other form of sport. It is part shooting, part mountaineering. You have to keep a sure foothold in case a bird gets up, keeping your eyes peeled for game, yet always watching lest your barrels should be dashed against a rock. A ptarmigan hill is a dangerous place for a best London gun.

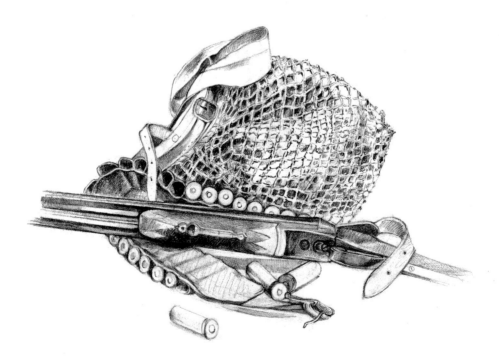

Cairngorm landscape – the haunt of ptarmigan and
(*inset*) the ptarmigan shooter and his dog

The twilight world of the Arctic tundra is home to one of our most unusual game birds. From the Aleutian islands, by way of a broad sweep through Siberia, northern Scandinavia, Greenland, Iceland and Arctic Canada down to our own Scottish highlands lie the haunts of the white grouse, snow grouse or ptarmigan. It is not a bird which is generally encountered by the average British sportsman, though perhaps the occasional party of grouse shooters, dogging the tops of some Scottish hill or walking up the craggy moorland margin where heather and bilberry give way to rocky scree, might catch a glimpse of the ghostly white outline of a ptarmigan as an outlying covey is flushed from a tumble of boulders.

The simple fact is that ptarmigan inhabit some of the most inhospitable territory in these islands. The Scottish highlands may not nudge the Arctic Circle, but at high altitude the mountain environment is similar to that of the northern tundra, a desert of frost-shattered rock and ice, of lichen and crowberry, of bilberry and the odd storm-stunted dwarf birch. Only the hardiest birds and animals can survive here, and the ptarmigan shares its home with little more than the soaring golden eagle. It is uniquely adapted to a harsh, hostile environment where the brief northern summer sees the blossoming of but a few poor scraps of vegetation amongst the rocks, and winter brings nothing but relentless snow and biting wind.

In the far north of Scotland around Cape Wrath the ptarmigan can be found as low as six hundred feet above sea level, but its highland strongholds throughout most of Scotland are the mountain peaks which tower to three thousand feet or more. Here the birds survive in self-contained populations which rarely travel far from their own rocky hilltops. For ptarmigan are well able to survive the winter snows, often burrowing deep into the drifts to find green shoots or berries upon which to feed, though sometimes, when the weather is particularly severe, the birds do migrate downhill to more hospitable territory.

Yet it is amongst the snow and rocks that the ptarmigan is truly at home. As its scientific name *Lagopus mutus* implies, it is one of the few birds which changes colour with the seasons. In summer, the plumage is a gorgeous patchwork of subtle greys and browns which blend into the surrounding rocks, making a close-sitting ptarmigan almost impossible to spot amongst the scree. As autumn sets in, more and more of the grey feathers are moulted, to be replaced by white until by the onset of winter the bird blends with the snowy landscape, save for its black tail feathers and brilliant red wattle, features which are retained the whole year round.

A few years ago I used to visit a certain Scottish grouse moor each August. Set amidst the glory of the Grampians, it spread its purple carpet high above the waters of Loch Rannoch and lay in the shadow of the mighty peak of Schiehallion, from the top of which on a clear day you can see from coast to coast clean across Scotland. Or so it is reputed. Clear days are at something of a premium on the top of Schiehallion. Even in August the mountain is usually wreathed in cloud and I have never had the chance to test the story.

This particular moor is not the sort of place on which a grouse shooter survives for very long if he is unfit. There were never really enough birds to make a driven day worthwhile, and the bulk of our shooting was walked up. We would cover miles of rough moorland in the course of a day's sport, negotiating the toughest and most spectacular terrain, often with one end of the line of guns three or four hundred feet above the other. Shooting under these conditions sometimes produces the most amazingly high curling birds which are the very devil to hit, but very satisfying when you do. It also requires a great deal of stamina, and of necessity our party of eight guns was young and fit.

The highlight of the week's sport was always a day at the ptarmigan. In this part of Scotland the white grouse are not often to be found below the three thousand foot contour, and though just once or twice when walking up the grouse we heard the korr korrk of a ptarmigan calling high up in the rocks above us, it took a special expedition to the mountain tops for us to get on terms with this elusive quarry.

Today's sportsman is so often mollycoddled. The pheasant shooter is regularly delivered to his peg by an air-conditioned Range Rover, and even the gentleman stalker generally manages to thumb a lift from a passing argocat. Not that I have anything against argocats; they have revolutionised the backbreaking business of getting deer off the hill and so have made life much easier for the professional stalker.

But there is one way and one way alone to get to the ptarmigan rocks, and that is on Shanks's pony. A friend of mine once took a couple of American guns out ptarmigan shooting with him, both of them young, fit and mad keen on their shooting, but better adapted to life in the comfortable surroundings of a Manhattan office than to the rigours of a Scottish mountain. When they asked him to point out the country which they were going to shoot, he indicated to them, with a broad sweep of his hand, the crags towering majestically above them.

'Jeez! You don't expect us to go up *there*,' came the horrified reply.

The next hour was spent investigating the possibility of argocats, ponies, even helicopters, but in the end the climb had to be made on foot. Even then, these two city boys felt utterly lost atop the mountain without their *Wall Street Journal* and hand-portable telephones.

Our ptarmigan day was going to be a tough one for men and dogs alike. All was bustle in the shooting lodge from early that morning. Guns and cartridges were made ready before breakfast, together with lightweight waterproof gear in case the weather proved foul. Boots needed to be cleaned and oiled. Then it was time for a shooters' breakfast of porridge followed by grilled snipe on toast, the snipe being the result of an exciting afternoon spent about the margins of a reed-girt loch on the fringes of the estate.

Before meeting up with Donald, the keeper who looked after our moor, there was a final veterinary inspection. Four days of hard graft across forbidding country had taken its toll on dogs as well as guns, and it was clear that the ptarmigan rocks would be no place to take an unfit dog. I took a long, hard look at Curly, my black labrador, and was forced to admit that her pads and more particularly her nipples were raw from unaccustomed and relentless exposure to the rasping heather. Sadly, I decided that it would be better for her to take a day's rest. She took it badly and expressed her displeasure in the way dogs do, namely by way of a steaming pile in the middle of the living-room carpet.

Donald arrived with the Land-Rover on the dot of eight o'clock, with the sun already climbing into a sky which was cloudless save for a few wreaths of pink and golden altocumulus. The air was sweet and there was every promise of a glorious day, though the forecast hinted that things might change during the course of the afternoon. Three miles of highland roads took us to the moor gate, and for another few hundred yards the Land-Rover bumped along an unmade track before lurching to a halt beside a stream. From here on we were walking.

The river was a delight. Across a rocky bed the gin-clear water tumbled, swirling in small pools which had the fishermen amongst the party twitching nervously with some curious withdrawal symptom. Mostly it was only a few inches deep, but streams such as these can be deceptive. Just two or three hours of heavy rain in the hills will turn every gulley and gutter into a foaming white streak against the dark rocks and heather, filling the rivers and turning them from innocent little watercourses to raging torrents that can sweep away a Land-Rover whose driver ventures unwisely to take a short cut home.

At first the track wound through a small ravine clothed in rowan and birch, with moss-covered rocks tumbling down to the stream below. Just the sort of place to find a black grouse, and we were to bag a couple of grey hens there later on in the week. But before long the way led out onto the open moor, steepening all the time and heading for the towering rocks ahead. The honeyed smell of flowering heather and the faint rankness of the moorland grasses, assailed our senses. From somewhere above came the stirring 'Go back, go back back back' of a grouse. It was wonderful to be on the moor once again.

Still the stream was our guide, and now we climbed up through the heather in silence: conversation flags fast as the work rate increases, the heart pounds and breath comes short. But just now and then there was a chance to sink into the heather and look back at the glorious sight of the highlands spread out below, to enjoy the somnolent hum of bees busying amongst the purple bells and to feel the warm sun against our faces. Then all too quickly Donald was on his feet again, striding onwards and upwards in his lean and economical way.

Soon we were through the two and a half thousand foot contour and the continuous heather gave way to rocks and bilberry clumps – a delicious source of sustenance when it was time once again to slump exhausted to the ground and take a breather. The last break was by a flowing spring, the source of that very stream which we had followed uphill for so long. Even at the height of the driest summer that spring never dries up, and always the water is icy cold, just the thing when you have climbed around two thousand feet.

It was time to line out. We were still climbing, but the first stage of Donald's plan involved working out a boulder-strewn ridge which would bring us out on the eastern lip of Coire Glas, a dramatic amphitheatre of loose scree gnawed out of the mountain's north-eastern flank. On the left was Mike, leader of the party, whose job it would be to swing clockwise around the back of the corrie; Donald directed operations from the middle of the line and I was on the right, with Matthew and David, my two neighbouring guns, seventy or eighty feet above me.

We had not gone far before there was a clatter ahead of me from a struggling bilberry clump and up jumped a red grouse. I tumbled it smartly onto the rocks below and, at two thousand eight hundred feet, I reckoned it must have been amongst the highest grouse in Scotland. At least we would not go home empty-handed, I thought with some relief. There were magnificent views of Ben Nevis, some thirty miles to the west, from the lip of Coire Glas, but none of us had yet spied a ptarmigan. Donald was fairly confident that there would be birds ahead of us in the big corrie, however, and the right-hand guns set off across the rocks in eager anticipation.

Shooting a corrie is something quite unlike any other form of sport. It is part shooting, part mountaineering. You have to keep a sure foothold in case a bird gets up, keeping your eyes peeled for game, yet always watching lest your barrels should be dashed against a

Clouds over the mountain tops

rock – a ptarmigan hill is a dangerous place for a best London gun. The first action came from above. A double shot rang out, then two singles as a white covey swept round the corrie and away over the summit ridge. I could see that Mike had at least one bird down, and Donald brought the line to a halt while the game was picked.

Then it was our turn. I spotted three birds twenty yards ahead, running amongst the rocks. As I brought my gun to readiness the covey jumped, seven birds in all, but I was unsteady on my feet and only got off one barrel. Above me, Matthew was onto them and between us we had a brace of ptarmigan down.

The rest of the corrie was blank, and, coming over the western lip, the reason why became clear. There was a pair of eagles circling high out over the ridge. Donald cursed. It was obvious that the north-western flank of the summit would be blank, for every sensible ptarmigan would have headed elsewhere for safety. However, eagles can sometimes be a blessing in disguise. Quite apart from the grandeur which they bring to the mountain tops, in this particular case there was every reason to believe that the refugee coveys would be waiting for us round on the south side of the mountain. Hope was not yet abandoned.

Reaching the western edge of the hill by lunch time, we encountered another two coveys and several pairs or singletons. There was some exciting snap shooting all down the line, with some extraordinarily difficult shots, and as we settled to eat our sandwiches, poised high above a spectacular scene of distant lochs and mighty peaks and with the sweet scent of highland air in our nostrils, five brace of ptarmigan plus my grouse were safely in the bag.

But there was every sign that the glorious weather was breaking. Already a streamer of cloud was extending from the summit above and banks of grey were moving up the glen. By the time that the signal came to line out for the long sweep around the southern side of the mountain, the cloud was threatening. A few dozen yards further on and I could see the mist, like a great grey blanket, sweeping uphill from my left, blotting out the light and seconds later enveloping us in its clammy grasp. Visibility was soon down to fifty yards.

Each of us took note of Donald's instructions in case of poor visibility: close up the line and maintain contact with your neighbouring guns. A curious business, since the mist now deadened all noise and made a conversation sound as though it was taking place inside a cardboard box. Yet although conditions were now far from perfect, there were plenty of ptarmigan in evidence. A pair erupted from below the rocks over which Murray, above me and to my left, was scrambling. I killed one, fluffing the second shot with bad timing. Within seconds a covey exploded at our feet and curled back into the wind over our heads. They were high, fast-driven birds with a stiff breeze under their tails and it was hard to see them through the murk, but Murray scrambled one shot which struck its mark.

The rocks were by now hellishly slippery, and I had a terrible job keeping my footing, ensuring that my gun was pointing in a safe direction, preventing it from getting dented on the unforgiving granite and keeping my eyes peeled into the mist at the same time. Muffled shots came from the left. Then a covey burst out of the boulders right in front of me. I killed the first cleanly, then stumbled and almost fell as the rock on which I was precariously poised tipped sideways. Sliding to the left and regaining my balance, I dropped to one knee on the rocks, reached for the choke barrel and took a second bird as the covey disappeared from sight. The tail bird in the pack staggered and crashed into the scree fifty yards ahead of me. A sense of elation greeted my first right and left at ptarmigan.

A fine drizzle was now falling out of the swirling cloud and I reached for the Barbour coat which I had carried for such an eventuality, rolled tightly and slung across my back. Quickly I slipped it over my tweed shooting jacket. Just in time, for it was clear that there were more ptarmigan about, now sitting tight until the last minute before jumping and curling away downhill. A pair broke on my left, but I was too slow and my shot slapped harmlessly into the rocks behind them. Murray was more successful, dropping the rearmost bird with his single shot.

More shots came from above, and as the visibility lifted to a hundred and fifty yards I could see the top half of the line halt while Donald worked his dogs across the rocks. The two springers were old hands at the game and were soon onto what was obviously a runner. For an inexperienced dog, picking ptarmigan off a mountain is no easy matter, as a wounded bird – or even a dead one for that matter – will often drop into a tiny crevice between the boulders and remain completely out of mark. However, the dogs did their work like true professionals, and within five minutes the missing bird was brought to hand.

With the bulk of the ptarmigan beat covered, and no sign of any let-up in the weather, Donald and Mike decided that we should start dropping down towards the march wall. How easy it was to be going downhill once more! All those hard-won feet of altitude seemed to slip away in a matter of moments, and before long we were into old heather and away from the ptarmigan rocks. Then, suddenly, we broke through the cloud base and the brown and purple patchwork of moorland stretched out once more below. Here the blackened stumps of freshly burnt heather, there a cushion of brilliant purple with the whitened twigs of the old heather sticking through, all interspersed with the emerald green of the bog moss which covered those treacherous peaty flushes into which a man might sink up to his knees – or worse.

A hare got up just in front of me, one of the blue hares common in this part of the highlands. A shot at a hare at the beginning of the day is unwise. There is a strict rule amongst walked-up grouse shooters that he who shoots a hare carries it, a rule which I learned through bitter experience on the very first morning upon which I walked a grouse moor. On that occasion I shot a large jack hare within half a mile of leaving the Land-Rover and was obliged to cart it about in my game bag for the rest of the day. But downhill and homeward bound it seemed a reasonable enough shot, so I swung onto the fast-fleeing form. My first shot was several feet behind, then as I fired the choke barrel the hare jinked behind a peat hag and was gone.

Inevitably, as I broke my gun to reload, a covey of red grouse rose at my feet. Struggling desperately for cartridges, I jammed one into the left chamber, snapped the gun shut to take a hurried line on one of the tail birds, and pulled the wrong trigger. By the time I had recovered my composure, the birds were gone, skimming low over the contours and away into the distance like surface-hugging missiles.

At four o'clock the shooting party reached the Tullochmeall march wall. We had been walking for the best part of seven hours, two of them in cloud and drizzle, and between us had shot ten brace of ptarmigan, a brace and a half of red grouse and a hare. Never believe it when someone tells you that ptarmigan shooting in the highlands is easy. Exhausting, exhilarating, challenging, even nerve-racking it might be, but never easy.

Now the flat grey clouds above us were once again starting to break up, and it was possible to glimpse once more the rocky crags far above. They seemed so distant, so

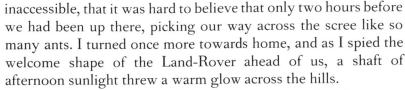

inaccessible, that it was hard to believe that only two hours before we had been up there, picking our way across the scree like so many ants. I turned once more towards home, and as I spied the welcome shape of the Land-Rover ahead of us, a shaft of afternoon sunlight threw a warm glow across the hills.

For several more seasons I shot on that moor and each year we had a crack at the ptarmigan, barring one in which the weather was so awful that it would have been just too much of a risk getting onto the rocks. Over the years the grouse numbers declined, and then Donald left to get a keepering job down south. At the same time the forestry boys moved in. The hillsides were ploughed with great furrows or 'grips' and the lands in between were planted up with sitka spruce.

It is a slow and painful death which has afflicted so many wonderful sporting estates in Scotland. First the grouse decline, probably because of a simple dip in the natural cycle of population. This reduces the income to the estate, which in turn decides to cut back on the keepering. With fewer keepers, the heather is no longer burnt as it should be and the 'patchwork quilt' of different aged blocks of heather in which the grouse can alternately feed, rest or find cover for their young, starts to deteriorate into a wasteland of long, rank heather which is good neither for sheep nor grouse. At the same time, foxes and other vermin take advantage of the lack of keepering, and before long the grouse have a struggle to survive in any numbers. It is a simple equation: the poorer the habitat, the fewer the grouse.

With income from shooting at an all-time low, the estate can only look to other forms of economic activity to make the place pay for itself, and in come the foresters and the intensive sheep graziers. More trees split up the few remaining blocks of moorland and provide yet more cover for foxes, while the sheep graze out the best heather. A depressing story, but all too evident on many highland estates, and it would be so in many more were it not for the dedication of those hill keepers who remain and the determination of some moor owners to keep up the grouse moor management even through the lean years.

However, although grouse have suffered a decline in that part of the highlands over the last ten years, ptarmigan have held their own. Indeed, there is every indication that their numbers have increased. After all, they are not affected by moorland management, their harsh and forbidding habitat has remained virtually undisturbed and their only enemy apart from the very occasional ptarmigan shooter remains the eagle and perhaps the odd high-altitude fox.

Only the development of the Scottish skiing industry has intruded upon the lofty home of the white grouse, and it seems that the birds have, in some places at least, come to terms with their new human neighbours. Even though the ski lifts have opened up access to the mountain tops for hill walkers in summer as well as the winter ski parties, the ptarmigan do not appear to be suffering any adverse reaction.

Ultimately, however large the growth in tourism, there will always remain hundreds of square miles of ptarmigan country which is virtually deserted, and in which the white grouse can prosper and flourish undisturbed. Scotland, thankfully, is a big place.

HARVEST FESTIVAL

Field, foreshore and hedgerow have a wealth of gifts to offer, and the wildfowler, rough shooter or hunter has far more chances than most people to tap into nature's bounty, for he is out in the countryside at all hours of the day and has the opportunity to venture into places which the average walker will never see.

The pumpkins, marrows, golden apples and sheaves of wheat which decorate parish churches up and down the land are as sure a sign as any of the turning of the seasons. Each year on the appointed date the aisle is bedecked with fruit and flowers, little bunches of carrots and courgettes catch the long shafts of autumnal sunshine which filter through stone mullioned windows, and brightly painted hips and haws line the choir stalls, a reminder that the harvest is not confined solely to those fruits for which man has toiled throughout the preceding twelve months, nor is it for his benefit alone.

Harvest festival is a special occasion for any rural community, an event which, even in this day and age when only a tiny minority of the British population actually works on the land, cements once more the link between village and countryside, between man and the soil which sustains him. Yet today the traditional timing of the harvest festival seems to bear little relationship to the gathering of the cereal crop which it was originally supposed to celebrate. In the breadbasket of eastern England there are few places nowadays where the combines are not rolling by the second week in August, and in a dry summer the winter sown barley is safely in the grain store before July is dead in the diary. By the time the harvest hymns ring out, next year's corn is already standing inches tall above the surface of the rich autumn earth.

It just shows how early sowing, new crop varieties and modern tackle at harvest time have left the church calendar hopelessly out of date – it is barely two generations since the labouring gangs toiled and sweated to bring in the year's corn crop by the time the apples ripened in early October. There were few country people who were not in some way connected with the land – or of course the sea, as was the case in the small Essex waterside parish where I spent five happy years. It is, or at least it was, a place where the traditions of farming and fishing go hand in hand, where local families as a matter of course have one foot in the water and the other in the heavy Essex clay. When the familiar words of 'We plough the fields and scatter' floated out over the churchyard wall and down towards the September salt marsh, purple with sea lavender and alive with the piping of whimbrel and oystercatcher, the church was hung with fishing nets as well as sheaves of wheat.

There was only one part-time fisherman left in the village then, where forty years previously there must have been a dozen. He it was who first showed me my way about the estuary in search of wigeon, and his punt and mine lay gunnel to gunnel, sleek and grey on the mud at low water in the village creek. David was from an ancient Tollesbury family of fowler-fishermen, men who spent the summer netting mullet, dabs and herrings, or maybe filling in with a spot of farm work, and who in winter attended to the oyster layings when they were not afloat in their open Essex gunning punts.

Perhaps, with his fishing boat and fowling punt, he really belonged to another age, or maybe the way of life was so bred into him that he maintained it out of a sense of loyalty to past generations. Either way, I still have a high regard for his philosophy towards fishing, fowling and the fruits of land and sea. It was an attitude which regarded the estuary as a living from which a variety of harvests were to be taken, each according to its season, to be added to the balance sheet of the family budget. Whether it was ducks and geese on a frosty January morning, flatfish at the back end of August, or simply a bag of driftwood picked up after a week of storms, the river was there to provide, to yield up its fruits to those who cared to seek them and, more to the point, who knew what they were looking for and how to find it.

After yet another unsuccessful trip after wigeon and teal, David would produce a large canvas bag and proceed to fill it with mussels, or draw up his punt at the foot of the sea wall and start to gather the sea spinach which grows there in profusion. 'Don't you go home empty-handed, bor,' he would say as another handful of winkles or a length of discarded rope went into that capacious side bag. It brought a whole new meaning to the phrase 'blank day', because of course a day spent along the estuary or indeed anywhere in the countryside need never be entirely blank.

That is something the older generation of professional fowlers and countrymen took for granted but which has been lost to us latter-day amateurs. 'Surely you can't eat *those!*' said an incredulous wildfowling friend whom I took down to the river for a day. We had chased a few parties of mallard about for most of the morning in the gun punt, but they weren't having any of it. Having rested on a mud bank far down river to eat our sandwiches and drink from our Thermos flasks, we waited for the tide to turn. I, as usual, had taken with me a plastic carrier bag and was in the process of collecting mussels. They looked filthy and disgusting, I will agree; covered with weed, barnacles and nasty, gritty mud, they appeared about as unappetising as any seafood imaginable. But when scraped clean with a good, strong kitchen knife and left to soak overnight in a bucket of water with a handful of oatmeal thrown over them, I knew that they would be delicious. My friend took some convincing, but eventually he too picked up a bag and started filling it with mussels.

Rarely do I come back from a wildfowling trip without a supply of seafood of some sort. In winter the mussels are at their best, down on the furthest muds at dead low water. There amongst the rusting plates of an ancient wreck, blown asunder by the RAF during wartime target practice, are the biggest, fattest mussels you could ever wish for.

If you are lucky and know what you are looking for, you may also find oysters, both the traditional 'natives' and the new-fangled Pacifics, the 'Rock oysters' which fetch a fortune in the wine bars of Belgravia. Oysters used to be a central part of the diet around the coast in centuries past – as witness the enormous piles of oyster shells which are regularly found when a cottage kitchen midden is excavated – but over the years they have developed from an everyday staple into a luxury dish. In terms of volume, the traditional oyster fisheries in Kent and Essex have thus long been in a state of decline. Recently they were hit especially hard by the side effects of the antifouling paints used by the pleasure craft with which the oyster fishermen share the tidal rivers. The antifouling preparations contain the poisonous tributyl tin and are expressly designed to inhibit the growth of barnacles on a boat's hull, so it is not surprising that they affected other shellfish as well. Thankfully the TBT problem was identified and tackled before the oystermen gave up the job altogether, and there are now signs of new life within the industry. But commercial fishing aside, it is still possible to pick up the odd wild native oyster along the low water mark, together with a few Pacifics that have been lost from the oyster fisheries in storm or tempest. They make a real treat, arrayed seductively on a bed of seaweed and topped with a twist of lemon.

At the beginning of the wildfowling season the samphire is still worth picking, before it turns yellow. Samphire or glasswort, so-called because it was once used by the glass-making industry, is at its best in July and August. The succulent green branching spikes can be found around the edge of the salt marsh at about the high water mark, and have long been a favourite amongst those who live along the coast. In some places it used to be gathered commercially and sold in bunches to the summer visitors, but it is several years

since I have seen samphire offered for sale at the roadside and these days it is probably considered more trouble to pick than it is worth. Some people like to pickle samphire, but I prefer it fresh, lightly boiled for five minutes in fresh water – no need to add salt, for it is salty enough already – and served with a knob of butter, rather after the manner of a plate of asparagus. There is nothing better as an accompaniment to the first duck of the season.

The sea spinach to which David first introduced me is also at its best in summer, although it can be gathered well into the autumn. It is the wild ancestor of the beet family, and produces a rich crop of dark green, waxy-looking leaves which clothe the salty soil above the tideline. Often it will be found growing on a sea wall or some similar embankment, where it remains largely ignored by those who walk their dogs along the coast path. Yet it has a flavour far richer and deeper than that of ordinary commercially grown spinach, which it closely resembles when cooked. And it's free, there for the picking. Like samphire, it should be washed, lightly boiled and served with butter.

Below the sea wall, amongst the wreaths of bladder wrack, is a harvest of winkles. One old boy from the village used to come down virtually every day to pick them, with an ancient two-wheeled hand-cart which he took along the tideline. As soon as he had collected a reasonable quantity of winkles, then he would be off to the local fishmonger to whom he would sell them. But there were plenty of other exciting things which ended up in that hand-cart. Driftwood for example. It really surprises me how few people make use of driftwood. Not just the good stuff, the odd plank of mahogany which gets washed ashore from a wrecked boat and is carefully dried and secreted at the back of the garage to await some special construction project, but the scraps as well. So many people have wood burning stoves today that one might think of driftwood as a convenient free source of fuel. Living beside the estuary it is possible to keep a cottage heated for an entire winter on driftwood, provided you know where to look for it, and are prepared to take a boat out to the hidden little bays, exposed to the wind and tide, where the stuff collects.

So much for the harvest of the estuary. Above the sea wall the countryside has a wealth of goodies to offer and the wildfowler, roughshooter or hunter has far more chance than most people of tapping into nature's bounty, for he is out in the countryside at all hours of the day and has the opportunity to venture into places which the average walker will never see. Where the partridges dust on the edge of the September stubbles, so the brambles hang luscious with blackberries and scores of small birds lift with a chatter as you move in to gather just sufficient to make that prince amongst puddings, blackberry and apple pie. Fresh blackberries, thinly sliced Bramley apples and a short, buttery pastry crust topped with cream – what a satisfying way to round off a Sunday dinner. Everyone has his or her own special blackberrying spot, but the best, most succulent fruit often seems to grow in the more shaded areas, perhaps just inside a wood or along a forest ride where there is a little more moisture available to make the berries swell.

Perhaps along the bramble hedge there is a crab apple tree, laden with small red and yellow fruit. Though bitter to the taste when raw, crab apples have a wonderful, almost scented flavour when cooked, and are well worth collecting if you get the chance. Crab apple jelly is the perfect complement to game and wildfowl and more delicate in flavour than the redcurrant jelly with which game is often served. A variation on the theme of plain crab apple is crab apple and elderberry jelly, a condiment which retains the subtlety of crab apple but which is spiced up with the unmistakable flavour of elder. Be careful not to use more elderberries than are necessary to add extra colour and piquancy, for otherwise they will swamp the delicate taste of the apples.

Nothing can be more redolent of early June than the scent of elderflower in the hedgerows, the creamy white dishes of florets a-buzz with insect life. A family favourite at this time of year is elderflower ice cream, flavoured with a syrup made by boiling up elderflowers and sugar. Once made, the syrup can be stored in a freezer, so that wonderful flavour of early summer can be enjoyed for several months afterwards.

Another hedgerow fruit which is frequently ignored is the bullace, a species of wild plum. When they ripen in late September, bullaces turn a honey yellow in colour and are quite delicious, though somewhat hard to collect as they insist on growing in the topmost branches along the hedgerow. It is a matter of either undertaking a prickly and uncomfortable climb, or waiting for the fruit to fall and then hoping that you are going to be first on the scene when it does so.

There is probably more folklore surrounding the preparation of sloe gin than any other hedgerow liquor, and perhaps that is not so surprising for there are no home-made liqueurs to match it, save perhaps an exceptionally good cherry brandy. Recipes for sloe gin abound, each prescribing different quantities and types of sugar, and different proportions of sloes to gin. Some enthusiasts have spent years perfecting what they believe to be the ultimate formula, the results of which are produced on shooting mornings or consumed in front of a blazing log fire after a hard day in the open air.

It is often reckoned that sloes are not ready for picking until they have had the first frost upon them. Then the dusty blue skins start to wrinkle and crack, so allowing the full flavour of the fruit to permeate throughout the gin. Those who cannot wait for nature to play her part pick their sloes early and put them in the freezer. In fact it is not necessary for the sloes to be frosted, and there is no doubt that storing them for any length of time in freezer or refrigerator adversely affects the flavour. Instead, the sloes may be pricked all over, traditionally a task accomplished with a silver fork. This was because the acid in the sloes reacted with the metal of an old-fashioned steel fork and left an unpleasant taste which could be transferred to the final product. Today, stainless steel has effectively overcome that problem.

Another misconception is that sloe gin made in October is ready for drinking by Christmas. It is no such thing. Not only does it take a good six months to infuse properly, but the liqueur will continue to mature for several years in storage. The longer you can leave it the better, and some of the best I have tasted has been well over ten years old.

Sadly the British climate does not seem to favour the development of good quality hedgerow nuts. Only in an exceptionally warm summer is there a superabundance of really good nuts, and in most years the kernels are small and barely worth the picking. However, it is possible to get a decent basket of nuts off the hazel, and fresh hazel nuts are, not surprisingly, far superior to those which are imported at around Christmas time. Once in a while there is also a good crop of chestnuts which can be gathered where they fall in the woods, their glossy brown skins peeping out from beneath a prickly green overcoat as they lie amongst the curling brown and yellow leaves.

Roast them in front of the fire on winter evenings, or if you think that's rather too messy a business, cook them in a low oven, but mind that each nut is pierced to let out the steam or they will explode with great force, sending powdered chestnut around your living-room or kitchen. Alternatively chestnuts can be blanched, cooked and eaten as a vegetable or purée. The secret here is to remove the bitter-tasting inner skin, best accomplished by scoring all the way round the outer shell before blanching the nuts in boiling water. With luck, the skin will then peel away relatively easily. But it is a tedious business preparing chestnuts, and so much simpler just to roast them.

Although the chestnut wood is only good for one decent crop of nuts every few years, each autumn will see an abundance of fungi, arrayed in every shade of red, white, blue, yellow and brown, bursting from the forest floor or clinging to the mossy, decaying stump of some ancient tree. The British are not on the whole very good at their fungi. Our conservative tradition encourages the consumption of little more than the common field mushroom and dismisses everything else as suspicious-looking toadstools.

Admittedly, fresh field mushrooms are delicious. I fill my pockets with them whilst out for early mornings with the beagles or when cubhunting with the foxhounds, picking them from the old pastures when they are at their tender best, still spangled with dew, then cooking them directly upon my return home and serving them up with eggs and bacon for breakfast. There are not so many fields now where mushrooms are to be found in plenty. Once again, changes in farming practice are responsible, for rotational grassland and arable cropping have largely replaced the old permanent pastures which were rich in mushrooms and so many other plant species besides. But here and there one does still come across a mushroom field, especially on grass where horses have been kept for a number of years. It is also worth looking out for the giant puffball, which inhabits similar surroundings to the field mushroom. This white, football-shaped fungus can be sliced like a loaf of bread and then fried in butter or dripping.

But the culinary Cinderellas of the fungus world are to be found in chestnut and birch woods at almost any time throughout the autumn: chanterelles, those apricot-hued trumpets of succulence, two or three inches in height; and it is best to look for them two or three days after rain has dampened the forest floor, when hopefully a fresh crop will be in evidence. Once you have learned to recognise them from their shape, colour and scent, no other fungus can possibly be mistaken for a chanterelle, and no other fungus eats as well – it is easy to see why, on the continental markets, they are sold as an epicurean delicacy. Chanterelles seem to prefer the slightly denser shade of the woodland floor. One woodland which I have known for over thirty years used to produce the most wonderful crops of chanterelles when I was a child. Then it was coppiced and for ten or more years we barely found a single chanterelle there, despite diligent searching, year after year. In due course, however, the woodland has regenerated and the chestnut trees once again stand tall, casting their shadow across the leaf mould. Now there are as many, if not more chanterelles than there were when I first knew it, and my own children hunt through the chestnut leaves each autumn and fill bags and baskets to overflowing.

Some people like to make soups with chanterelles, but I find that a terrible waste. They should be enjoyed on their own, fried in butter with a few chopped onions and a little parsley, perhaps as a starter or as a side dish.

If it is soup you are after, then there is nothing to beat the boletus, which grows in much the same sort of habitat as the chanterelle, but which prefers if anything slightly more open woodland. All the boletus family have characteristic spongy gills under a reddish brown cap which might measure anything up to ten inches across, but only a couple of species are good to eat – and one, whose stem is tinged with red, can make you very ill indeed. Nevertheless, the real boletus enthusiast can bring back from a walk lasting a couple of hours sufficient fungi to make masses of the very finest mushroom soup or to flavour stews and casseroles over several weeks. For unlike chanterelles, boletus when cooked keeps well in the freezer.

Mother Nature has plenty of good gifts to offer, each providing rewards far in excess of their simple value as food or fuel. Nobody expects to live off the land today – to do so and yet to retain any reasonable standard of health and comfort would be extremely difficult, one might almost say impossible. But the countryman who picks and collects what nature has provided for him does not do so in order to maintain his own subsistence and that of his family, any more than the sportsman needs to shoot in order to keep his belly full. There are other people whose full-time job it is to produce food to fill the nations's larders. They're called farmers.

On the contrary, collecting nature's bounty might be considered just as much a recreation as is hunting, to use the word in its widest sense. Like hunting it requires a knowledge of natural history, not just the academic knowledge achieved by studying books, but a working knowledge, obtained by observation and experience. The rewards, too, are similar to the rewards that the hunter enjoys – appreciation and understanding of the countryside, its plants and its wild creatures, relaxation and escape from the routine of twentieth-century living, and perhaps some culinary delight at the end of it all. From the earliest times, hunting and gathering went hand in hand, and why should it not continue to be so today?

For the roughshooter or wildfowler who pursues a wild quarry in its own natural or semi-natural surroundings, a pocketful of mushrooms or a bunch of samphire is only a logical extension of the wigeon, pigeon or rabbit in his game bag, for that too has been gleaned from the countryside. When the proceeds of his labours are turned into a meal then the results are immensely satisfying, especially when the vegetables are home-grown and the Bramleys for the blackberry and apple pie come from his own tree. Such a feast, taken in the golden glow of autumn – the first game of the new season accompanied by home-grown produce and food from field and hedgerow – is in itself a sort of harvest festival, a rare opportunity to give thanks for all that nature provides for her friends and supporters, year in and year out.

HOBNAILED HUNTERS

Fell foxhunting is a sport the roots of which reach deep into Cumbrian history. Until he retired after forty seasons in hunt service, John Nicholson was huntsman to the Lunesdale, and held the honoured and revered position of senior huntsman amongst the fell packs.

On the fell top

On a Sunday afternoon in August the Lake District can resemble a cross between Blackpool's golden mile and a badly managed roadworks on the M25. When you finally succeed in edging through the snaking queues of cars, caravanettes and luxury continental coaches and worm your way into Grasmere or Hawkshead, you are confronted with a seething mass of camera-bearing, sunhat-wearing humanity so thickly wedged between the gift shop windows and the double yellow lines that it seems as though the visitors' honeypots are drowning in their own honey. A terrible thing is *Homo Touristicus*.

But come the autumn, when the summer visitors begin the great migration back to the towns, it is just possible to sense that behind Lakeland's tourist façade there beats a heart as old as the walls of Skiddaw slate. A heart of deeply sprung and heavily nailed fell boots, of a simple horn handle on a shepherd's neck-crook, of Herdwicks huddled against a stinging storm of winter sleet. The old way of life may have changed in recent years as it has done everywhere in our so-called civilised western world, thanks to American pulp television, Japanese cars and London money, but in the quieter backwaters of Cumbria, traditional community life is still breathing, cemented together by the Hill Livestock Compensatory Allowances and by foxhunting.

Hunting the fox is a sport the roots of which reach deep into Cumbrian history. Hounds were kept in these parts as far back as the seventeenth century, indeed the fleet-footed northern hounds were so much in demand that they were exported far and wide across the kingdom. Local people banded together to form their own small trencher-fed packs with which to hunt the deer, fox or hare, and by far the most celebrated of these was John Peel, he of the coat so grey. Perhaps the most well known figure in foxhunting folklore, Peel was no silk-hatted and swallowtailed gentleman on a Leicestershire hunter, but a small-scale Caldbeck farmer and horse dealer who hunted his hounds on foot or from the back of a sturdy pony. Today's fell foxhunters are, in spirit at least, his direct descendants.

Fell foxhunting is a sport which brings local people together like no other activity, but it is also a business with a serious side. In a sheep farming country, the fox is a pest of major proportions, particularly at lambing time, when all the hard work of the fell shepherd can be put to nought in a few minutes by a lamb-worrying vixen.

When the foxhunter of the shires justifies his sport on the grounds of fox control one can be excused for doubting whether he is telling the whole truth. Amongst the fells, though, fox killing is an essential activity which is carried out humanely yet efficiently by the hunts. Were hunting to cease in Britain, there are parts of lowland England where the fox would probably disappear within a few years. That would not be so in the fells, where hunting is virtually the only means of keeping the fox population in check.

There are six fell packs which hunt the hill country of Cumbria and its environs. They have a tradition all of their own, a character which is quite unique. Hounds are hunted on foot, for there is no other way in which they could be followed into the soaring crags and rocky screes of the fell country, where the foxes dwell far above the lonely farmsteads and stone-walled in-bye land around the valley heads. There is no pretension about a fell pack. Its support is drawn from the local farming population, whose loyalty to the hunt is cemented by the fact that even today, the fell packs operate on a trencher-fed principle, with hounds going back to the farms on which they were brought up when hunting ceases during the summer months.

Holding up hounds as the terriers do their work

Fell huntsmen of old: (*l to r*) Harry Hardisty (Melbreak); Walter Parkin (Lunesdale); Joe Wear (Ullswater); Anthony Chapman (Coniston); Johnny Richardson (Blencathra); Arthur Irving (Eskdale & Ennerdale)

The Central Committee of Fell Packs, formed in 1968 under the umbrella of the Masters of Fox Hounds Association to represent the Cumbrian foot hunts, is comprised of five old-established packs and one comparative newcomer. The Blencathra, Coniston, Eskdale and Ennerdale, Melbreak and Ullswater hunts all trace their establishments back to the last century or even earlier; the Lunesdale foxhounds are a relatively recent pack. Originally formed in the 1930s, the establishment was reorganised in its present form in 1948. Unlike almost every other hunt, the Lunesdale does not have a Master; instead it is a limited company with a council of management and a chairman, Malcolm Robinson, whose grandfather, Tom Robinson, hunted the hounds before the last war. That the system works to the satisfaction of all is evidenced by the support which the Lunesdale hounds receive, both from their own members and from the local community at large.

Much of that support and goodwill is engendered by the huntsman, whose official job may be that of keeping the hounds and killing foxes, but whose role goes far deeper, amounting almost to that of full-time PR man. Until the spring of 1990, when he retired after no less than forty seasons in hunt service with the Lunesdale, that job of huntsman was carried out by John Nicholson. At that time John held the honoured and revered position of senior huntsman amongst the fell packs, a post formerly occupied by such great names as Joe Bowman, Anthony Chapman and Joe Wear, mighty hunters celebrated in the song and legend of the Lakes.

John Nicholson – or John Nick, as he is known throughout the Lunesdale country and beyond – started hunting at a tender age. Almost as soon as he could walk, he was following the Coniston hounds, first under Ernie Parker and subsequently under Anthony Chapman, Parker's former whipper-in who took over as huntsman in 1944. Then in 1950 the job of whipper-in came up with the Lunesdale. John Nicholson applied and was taken on. His boss was Walter Parkin, who had whipped in to the hunt before the war and who had taken over as huntsman in 1948.

It was a great honour, but a tough apprenticeship. A fell hunting establishment is not a big one. There is no such thing as a kennelman to do the skinning or scrub down the yards, just a huntsman and a whip, and the whip usually ends up doing most of the dirty jobs. Nor does he even get to wear a scarlet coat. That privilege is reserved for the huntsman alone, the whip being clad in a coat of brown twill, though with scarlet cuffs and waistcoat.

'The first job a whipper-in has to learn is to listen to the huntsman. He does all the running around at the kennels, and does what he's told. I was whip for thirteen seasons until 1963 when Walter Parkin retired. Then I took the job on as huntsman and I've been there ever since,' said John, speaking shortly before his retirement.

Like all the other fell huntsmen, John was employed full-time by the hunt only during the winter months. In the summer he spent his time working on a farm or engaged in casual jobs like dry stone walling. Meanwhile, the hounds would be looked after on the farms where they were walked as puppies. This practice forges a close sense of identity between hunt supporters and the kennels, ensuring that hound walkers take a long-term interest in the progress of 'their' hounds – which in a sense are just that.

At the beginning of September all the hounds come back from the farms to a hound show at Sedbergh. Traditionally, a row of stakes was driven into the ground, to which the farmers tied their hounds for collection by the huntsman. That practice no longer continues, but the show is still one of the highlights of the hunt's year. That night, the hounds are brought back to the kennels, a group of whitewashed stone buildings high on a steep bank outside Sedbergh, and two days later they start hunting.

'They'll be out on the farms and then two days later they'll be hunting together as a pack. They never forget it, they just go out hunting as though they've been together all summer,' said John. 'We couple the puppies together for a few weeks. We take them hunting on couples, then when a fox gets up we slip the couples and let them go, you see. We do that as soon as we can rely on them to be safe with stock.'

Steadiness to livestock is something which is of vital importance to the fell foxhound, and it is something by which John Nicholson sets great store.

'A hound has got to be absolutely steady. I've seen an old hound start on sheep, I don't know why they do it, but I've seen them start. Once a hound has worried a sheep and he comes back into kennels the other hounds know. They'll all be smelling at it. They know, and they'll all start. So if you have a hound that does worry a sheep, it has to be put down or it'll ruin the lot of them.

'When Joe Wear came out of the army and went to the Ullswater the hounds were a bit wild. He didn't ken them, you see, as he'd been away for six years. The first morning they went out, they started to hunt sheep. Joe had to shoot sixteen of them that night'.

The fell foxes come down at night to the farms to feed, and during the day they return to the high ground to lie up, perhaps on a bank or hillside upon which there is a covering of bracken or heather, and from where there is a commanding view so that any approaching danger can be monitored. Therefore when the huntsman unkennels his hounds, his first object is to strike off the drag, or overnight scent trail of the fox, in the hope that this will lead him to the place where 'Charlie' has lain up for the day.

Sending his whipper-in high up onto the fell top, from where he might see the fox break cover and head for the high ground, the huntsman casts his pack with bellowed notes of encouragement which echo about the fells and which must set the hairs a-tingle down the spine of any fox which hears them. Then, moving ever upward with the effortless pace of one who has walked the fells since childhood, a pace which soon sorts out the unfit and turns even the average rambler's legs to jelly, he works towards the holding cover about the fell side, following up any drag which his hounds may have discovered.

When the hounds find their fox, they announce the fact with a roar of music, and the hunt begins. Fell foxhounds are a breed quite distinct and separate from their low-ground cousins, although it is believed that the two strains originated from the same common ancestral root. They are much lighter of bone than the foxhound of the shires, slightly smaller in height and much leaner in appearance. They are built for speed and agility, and are able to run all day across the unforgiving rocks of the Cumbrian hills. The fell hound is also of a rather paler colour than that which is more fashionable in the south, for the simple reason that a light coloured hound stands out well against the dark brown and orange of the hillside; as the pack latches onto the line of its fox, it is as though a string of pearls were spread out across the bracken, threading through the scree and over the top of the fell.

The foxes are different too, or at least they were in the days of the legendary 'greyhound' foxes. Lean, long-legged and flecked with grey about their coats, the greyhound foxes dwelt in the high ground. 'A greyhound fox would go all day, and he'd go straight away, not like a lot of foxes which just go round and round in circles. And he was big, the biggest we ever caught was twenty-four pounds. But you very seldom see a greyhound fox type today, they've died out, they have.

'In the old days, people never used to see a fox down in the low ground, they were always up on the fell. But now the foxes come down into the villages to visit the dustbins. They see that much of car lights, people and hikers that they're not bothered by them, they're more used to people these days.'

Fox catcher though he is, John Nicholson always insisted on fair play. He would never dig out a fox if he could help it. When a fox went to ground in a scree bed or 'borran', he would hold hounds back sixty yards or so and let the terrier men do their best to bolt it.

'I always try to kill a fox above ground, always give him a fair chance. We get far back enough from the hole, and always have done, but generally we catch them in the end. We caught eighty-eight last season and the same number the year before. Usually we catch between sixty and eighty, depending on the weather.'

The foxes in the Lunesdale country are renowned for being 'straight-necked' fellows, who will cover long distances during the course of a hunt. This is partly due to the type of country which is hunted, for the Lunesdale does not operate in the Lakes proper, but in the eastern part of Cumbria, plus a portion of Lancashire and North Yorkshire. It is big, open fell country, where the wide and forbidding mountains on the edge of the Pennines replace the more intimate landscape of central Lakeland. From Cross Fell in the north to Ingleborough in the south, with the town of Kendal along its western extremity, the

RIGHT
John Nicholson – forty years in hunt service

Lunesdale country exceeds four hundred square miles, and is one of the largest hunting countries in Britain. And yet all of it is covered on foot, and hounds know every square inch.

'I've known hounds go twenty mile any day, aye, that they have. And they can find their way about the fell right enough. We left one pup out after hunting one night down Kendal way, daftest pup as ever went into kennels, and next morning it was back at its walk at Horton in Ribblesdale, forty miles away. I've known times when most of them have been out all night, scattered about all over. They drop down to the farms, and we go out next day to pick them up.

'Of course it's much easier now, when you can just get into your motor car. We used to have to walk, aye. When I first started, we'd walk every place. Places twenty miles away we used to walk to the day before, ready for the next morning, and we'd kennel the hounds at a farm. And after we'd finished there, we'd walk on to the next village.

'There weren't any hound vans then. At night, when you'd finished hunting, you walked back straight over the fell with hounds, many times in the dark. When you tell them today they won't believe you.

'Mind you, in them days you could walk the roads because there was no traffic, you could go miles and hardly meet a car. Today you just can't walk at all on the roads.'

Those were quieter, simpler times, when a long walk across the fell tops by the light of the moon ended with the welcoming clatter of boots on the cobbled yard of a hill farm. Hounds were fed and bedded down in the warm circle of lamplight on fresh straw, the sweet smell and hoarse coughing of cattle beside them in a neighbouring stall, while the huntsman and whip relaxed over a tatie pot and pint of ale in the farmhouse parlour.

The hunt goes out in all weathers. Drenching rain, frost which shines like crystal from the bracken and picks out the fell tops in white rime before the sun rises, wild gales that make it almost impossible to hear hounds and which make walking difficult if not downright dangerous, swirling mist, and snow which sets the hills a-sparkling.

'We rarely miss a day, unless it is dense fog or a lot of snow. Thick snow is bad for the sheep, because they get stuck in it, and it's bad also when the becks are running heavy because the sheep can get washed away. Then the farmers worry, because the stock are worth a lot of money. They don't want you to hunt, and you can understand why. It's just plain daft going out in conditions like that, it's dangerous.'

Even when the weather is favourable, hunting in the mountains can be treacherous and accidents occur regularly to hounds, hunt staff and followers alike. Injuries can result from a fall amongst the slippery rocks, or perhaps when hounds, working far above, dislodge loose stones which come crashing down onto those below – John once had a narrow escape in such circumstances. He also recalls the occasion when two hounds fell down a thirty foot deep pothole. Walter Parkin was huntsman at the time, and, reaching the brim of the chasm, he spotted the two hounds on a ledge below him. A follower rushed to the nearest farm for a rope, and eventually Walter was gingerly let down into the pothole, from where he recovered them, safe and well.

Sometimes the outcome is not so happy. Terriers are particularly at risk amongst the deep rocky tunnels where the foxes lie. It is all too easy during a dig for a boulder to become dislodged, collapsing into the earth and either crushing the unfortunate terrier or blocking its escape. Under such circumstances the terrier men work round the clock, sometimes for days, to bring the dog out alive. On one occasion at Patterdale two terriers were entombed in a particularly deep earth. For five days the men dug in relays, and eventually one was brought out alive; the other was never seen again.

The risks are just as great for those who do the digging. To become pinned by a moving boulder, high up on a mountainside in winter and with dusk descending is no laughing matter. In cases of real emergency the mountain rescue service and even the RAF with their helicopters are brought into action.

The hounds continue regular hunting until around Easter, by which time lambing is in full swing up in the fells; the hill farms are then at their most vulnerable to predation by foxes, and this is when the foxhounds come into their own as a highly efficient pest control service. Those who dispute the fact that foxes kill young lambs should spend early spring in the fells, for in these parts a lamb-worrying fox is a menace. A vixen is often worse than a dog fox, and John Nicholson believes that a single vixen without cubs is the worst of all. He has seen ten lambs killed by such a fox in one night during the lambing season.

Any farmer who is having trouble with foxes at lambing time simply telephones the kennels, and the hounds will be out the following morning. When on lambing calls, John would only take out a few of his best and most experienced hounds with him, hounds which would hunt a line through a field of ewes and lambs.

'Aye, it's a risky job going amongst the young lambs, so we only take the steadiest of our hounds, usually about twenty of them.' Low-country hunters used to speaking of hounds in couples may find the practice of counting them individually somewhat foreign, but it is another example of the uniqueness, the individuality of Cumbrian hunting.

Lambing calls start early in the morning, at around five o'clock. Hounds are taken straight to the lambing field and unboxed, whereupon the huntsman will endeavour to get them to hit off the drag of the particular fox which has been causing a problem. Usually it does not take long, for at this early hour the drag is still fresh, and hounds are soon onto the line of their quarry. Quickly they take the drag up into the fell where Charlie has taken refuge after his night of feasting, and with luck they will rouse him from his slumbers.

'They nearly always catch a fox that's been lamb worrying, because he's usually got a full belly. They've tried other ways to get them, particularly those as are not hunting people, but hunting's the only way of catching foxes up in the hills, and they come back to us in the finish, most of them.'

The efficient nature of the service which the hounds provide to the hill farmer makes lambing time one of the busiest periods of the fell huntsman's calendar. Frequently he will be out on several consecutive mornings, answering a string of calls from farmers troubled by foxes. John remembers one season in which he went out on call for twenty-three mornings in a row, starting around five o'clock each day.

By the end of April lambing calls are over, and in May the huntsman is paid off for the summer. Not that John Nicholson would ever sit about and do nothing, mind you. Idleness does not come easily to an active man, and when he was not engaged in farmwork or walling, John always found some other occupation.

Terriers – tireless workers

Summer is also the season of the hound shows. Once Rydal was the only show at which fell hounds competed, and it is still reckoned to be the premier event in the hound show calendar where fell hounds are concerned, though Lowther is now a serious competitor.

'Everybody turns out for Rydal Show, it's a get-together. You meet all the people from all the other packs, and if you show hounds at Rydal and get a prize, then you've got a good hound. We won the championship a few times.

'Oh yes, it's a great day is Rydal, maybe not as good now as it used to be, because there's that many hound shows, and Lowther's definitely bigger.'

Lowther hound show developed from the equestrian driving trials held on the Lowther estate, formerly the home of the great Earl of Lonsdale, the 'Yellow Earl', so called because of the colour of his livery. Now classes are held for all sorts of hounds, and the event has become extremely popular with hunting folk.

During the summer, when he is not actually showing hounds, John often parades them at one or other of the local agricultural shows:

'Folk like to see the hounds at shows, and you get more people watching the hounds than looking at the cows and sheep.'

Once he had the privilege of taking the Lunesdale hounds to the premier agricultural show in Britain, the Royal Show at Stoneleigh in Warwickshire. In company with the other five fell huntsmen, all of whom had been invited to take part in a special parade, he travelled south.

'We went the night before, and we had quite a party', he says, in classic understatement. It is at such parties that another tradition of hunting in the fells is revealed, the tradition of song. Whether it be the evening after a hound show, a 'tatie pot' hunt supper or social night, or even the end of a particularly good hunting day when all are assembled in the bar of a local pub: when fell hunters are gathered together, they sing.

A hunting sing-song is a glorious celebration of the warmth, comradeship, and also the vitality and vigour of the fell packs. Though the singers in turn are afforded a respectful silence, each chorus is roared out by the company in tones fit to raise the roof, and interspersed where appropriate with whoops, hollas and the blowing of hunting horns. It is the very essence of that which binds together the hunters of these parts.

Hunting songs have been a feature of fell foxhunting for as long as anyone can remember. Epic hunts, favourite hounds and the exploits of celebrated huntsmen are all recorded in songs that are handed down through the generations. If the hounds have a particularly memorable day, then a song is written about it. There are old favourites, like 'The Six Fell Packs', or 'Joe Bowman' with its stirring chorus:

> When the fire's on the hearth and good cheer abounds
> We'll drink to Joe Bowman and his Ullswater hounds,
> For we'll never forget how he woke us at dawn
> With the crack of his whip and the sound of his horn.

But there are also dozens of new songs being constantly added to the repertoire, often written by those with little formal education or musical training. They are songs written from the heart, to be sung before an appreciative audience – some are quickly forgotten, but others go on to become well-loved 'standards' in their own right.

Like many of the great huntsmen before him, John Nicholson is celebrated in song, a ballad which hails the glories of the Lunesdale hunt and recounts the most famous moments of its huntsman of forty years' standing. After each verse comes the chorus:

> From Mallerstang to Brigsteer, from Littledale to Brough,
> From Hazelslack to far off Malham Dale,
> Bold Reynard he has hunted on Barbon's bracken lots
> And he's caught a fox on top of Wild Boar Fell.

Few doubt that even when John has gone to join Joe Bowman, Joe Wear and the others in that great hunting ground beyond the fell tops, those words will still make a merry commotion around the pubs of Cumbria.

It seems odd that this thriving oral tradition of hunting songs is something that has largely escaped the attentions of the folk song establishment. Today's traditional folk singer bases his repertoire largely on the records of the late nineteenth- and early twentieth-century folk song collectors, men like Cecil Sharp, one of the founding fathers of the English folk song revival. When Sharp stomped the countryside in search of the few greybeards who still remembered 'the old songs', he was all too well aware that he was playing the part of a museum keeper, capturing the dying echoes of a tradition already moribund, a culture which had all but withered in a fast changing countryside.

Yet here in the Lakes, almost a century on, there is a singing tradition which is still alive, still vibrant, still evolving, which does not rely on myths of rural arcadia or professional folk musicians to sustain it: it is born of and nourished by the wild sport of the fells. While there are yet foxes to be chased over Wild Boar Fell and while the music of hounds still rings out across Barbon's bracken lots, then the songs will continue to flourish. Should hunting ever cease, then there will be time enough to call in the folk song collectors.

John Nicholson leads the chorus at a hunting sing-song

Hunting in the fells has changed considerably since John Nicholson started following in the footsteps of Anthony Chapman. Perhaps the biggest difference today is the traffic; every road is now treacherous, and lanes which twenty years ago barely saw a car have been turned into racetracks which hounds and followers cross at their peril. The worst blow came with the construction of the M6, which sliced the Lunesdale country in two from top to bottom. It is a death trap to be avoided at all costs, and has effectively closed a swathe of country which was once crossed regularly by hounds during the season. On one occasion shortly after it was opened two were killed in an accident which left two cars slightly damaged, although thankfully there were no human casualties. But today the M6 is even busier, and John dreads the thought of a pile-up.

'If hounds got onto the motorway these days and there was a bad accident, we'd be straight off to London and there'd be an enquiry. We'd probably be told to keep thirty miles away, and that would just about stop hunting altogether.

'We have people watching the main roads and bypasses, but when hounds are running fast, it's a job to stop them. You can slow the traffic down with a red flag, but even then some drivers just don't take any notice.'

Motor cars have revolutionised hunting in another sense, for now many elderly followers who are no longer able to follow hounds across the fells on foot come out and follow by car. Where there are suitable roads with vantage points which look out across the mountains, hunting by car can be great fun. A good pair of binoculars and a map enables the car follower to keep up with the hunt for much of the day, and on some occasions he can find himself closer to the scene of the action than the footsloggers struggling far behind the flying pack.

There is another piece of modern technology which was formerly frowned upon but is now accepted as a part of life in the fells: the Citizens Band radio set. Even when hounds, huntsman and followers are separated by miles of rough country, they can now keep in radio contact. When there is a risk of hounds getting too close to a busy road then the radio is invaluable, for a car follower can be instantly despatched to a suitable place on the highway from which to stop hounds or warn approaching traffic. Equally, CB radio can be a life-saver in case of an emergency high up on the mountains. Yet some people do find it out of place in the hunting field, an intrusive, jarring and discordant reminder of the late twentieth century when set against the timeless picture of the scarlet-clad huntsman, hounds at heel, striding the hills in his iron-shod boots.

Now that he has come to the end of his time as huntsman, John Nicholson has time to reflect, time to watch the younger generation do their share of the hard work, although in the manner of old timers everywhere, he maintains that 'the young'uns today aren't the same as they were in the old days'.

'You just see the older folk out hunting regularly, but the youngsters are not following on as they used to. Of course in the olden days they hadn't got motor cars and so on.'

John plans to maintain his links with the hunt during his retirement. Whether watching a road or keeping an eye on some other place where hounds might be likely to come to harm, he intends to do his bit to help. And he intends to do it on foot.

'When I come to the end of my time, I'll be walking like, not in a car.'

But no doubt when the miles get long and the rain comes down in the sort of stair rods which only Cumbria can fashion, there'll be someone ready to offer him a lift.

A Stag
of Warrant

Far removed from the splendour of scarlet coats and polished boots, the harbourer's solitary world is that of the frosty bracken brake at first light and the lonely woodland ride. More than any man on Exmoor, he knows and loves the red deer.

Were hunting ever to be ended within the realm of England, there is one place which it is hard to believe would not seek secession from the Union. On the forest of Exmoor they would take to the hills and fight a rearguard action against the grey forces of officialdom. On the backs of a thousand hunt horses and ragged-maned moorland ponies would be mounted such a scarlet coated cavalry as would repulse Old Noll himself. With the sound of the accursed hunting horn ringing defiantly in his ears like some martial bugle, even the old arch-puritan would be forced to concede that it is not for nothing that the inns around Winsford and Withypool bear the emblem of the Royal Oak. And were the hated edict to be enforced upon Exmoor folk, then who knows what noises would wake the slumbering combes on a moonlit night – the clatter of hooves across a metalled track, the ringing cry of hounds across the common and from far off the thrilling note of a view holloa.

Horses, hounds and hunting are the lifeblood of Exmoor, that small heather and bracken-strewn patch of north Devon and west Somerset which rears above the Bristol Channel. From the days of the Saxon kings it has been a royal hunting ground, as the Domesday records confirm. Down the centuries Exmoor's Free Suitors remained guardians of its ancient forest laws until the time of Waterloo, when the Suitors were finally paid off with the grant of land and Exmoor was officially disafforested.

But still the hounds remained to hunt the fox and the hare. And they remained above all to hunt the wild red deer, the undisputed monarchs of these parts, recognised today in the emblem of the Exmoor National Park, that late twentieth-century version of the old Royal Forest in which ancient right is transmuted into the jargon of the civil servant and the part of the Free Suitors is acted out by the men from the Countryside Commission.

The red deer of Exmoor probably owe their present existence to hunting, which has continued around these parts since time immemorial with only one short break in the 1820s. It is the presence of the hunt, and the respect for the deer which hunting has engendered, which has ensured that the herd of up to a thousand animals has not merely survived but flourished, the only native wild herd in the whole of southern England.

It is only on Exmoor proper and the area immediately adjacent to it that the sport of staghunting is still practised in Britain today. The one other remaining deer hunt, the New Forest Buckhounds, pursues not the red but the fallow deer. A sport which rouses strong emotions amongst both its proponents and detractors, the hunting of the wild red deer with packs of hounds is a field sport unlike any other. It is akin on the surface to foxhunting, but although both activities are conducted from horseback by packs of hounds controlled by Masters and huntsmen who wear scarlet coats, there the similarity ends.

Where the object of the foxhunter is to find and hunt, or hunt and kill any fox, the staghunter's concern is the selective management of the red deer herd. There are allotted seasons in the year for stags and hinds, when the three West Country stag hunts – the Devon and Somerset, the Tiverton and the Quantock – will attempt to hunt and kill a certain number of stags of particular different age and qualities, and complete a hind cull. Once found, the chosen deer is hunted until brought to bay, at which point he turns to face his pursuers and is then shot at close range by one of the hunt staff. Though it is the Master or Masters of the hunt who are ultimately responsible for the deer management policy, the task of overseeing the job lies very much in the hands of one man, a man who is the eyes and ears of the hunt where deer are concerned, the harbourer.

Far removed from the splendour of scarlet coats and polished boots, the harbourer's solitary world is that of the frosty bracken brake at first light and the lonely woodland ride which the deer cross at night in order to feed on the farmer's root field. More than any man on Exmoor, he knows and loves the deer – throughout summer and winter he watches them, by his extraordinary skills of woodcraft he studies the hinds and tracks the stags. And it is his job to select and 'harbour', or locate, a stag to run before the hounds on a hunting morning. By tapping into his local network of informants he will find out where the deer are feeding and lying up, and the day before the meet he will go and look for a suitable stag. Then early the following morning, just as it is starting to get light, he will endeavour to intercept it as it returns from its nightly foraging and before it lies down to rest, so as to pinpoint its position for the huntsman.

Red deer hunting, like stalking with a rifle, is regulated according to the seasons. At the beginning of August, hounds will hunt the autumn stags, big, mature animals at the peak of their powers, which will use all their speed and cunning to deny the pack its reward. Autumn staghunting ceases at the end of October at about rutting time, when attention turns to the hind cull. In hind hunting no particular beast is selected prior to the meet; instead the pack is divided in two. Half is employed to split up the herd of hinds and push one away, whereupon the remainder of the hounds are laid on and the hunt begins. So during the winter the harbourer's skills are not needed. He starts work again in March, when it is time to hunt the spring stags – the younger stags, up to four years old. At the end of April, hunting is over for the summer.

The post of harbourer is an enormously important and respected one within the hunt, but it tends nevertheless to be an unpaid 'honorary' task, undertaken by someone whose devotion to hunting is matched only by his fascination with the deer. It is also a job which is steeped in country lore and fieldcraft, and is therefore one which comes easiest to those whose business takes them out into the fields and woods for a living. Several noted harbourers have been gamekeepers while others have made a living from farming around the fringes of Exmoor forest itself.

Ralph Slocombe

Nevertheless, some harbourers also worked for many years in hunt service, and one such man is Ralph Slocombe. Ralph learned the business of staghunting from the bottom up, as it were. In 1918 he entered the famous kennels of the Devon and Somerset Staghounds at Exford as kennel boy, the most lowly position in hunt service. But he stuck to the job, and before long became head kennelman, in charge of caring for the hounds under the watchful eye of the huntsman, who had overall command of the kennels. Slowly climbing the ladder he became second whipper-in, allowed to wear the coveted scarlet coat and to appear in the field on hunting days, and in the late thirties he finally took over as first whipper-in.

Life in kennels for the five paid staff was strict, and the huntsman's word was law. Ralph recalls that 'The huntsman was more like a gentleman in those days. He didn't do much, only hunt the hounds and walk them out in the afternoons. We whips would have to walk out with him to keep the hounds up together, and Colonel Wiggin, the Master would come and walk out with us'.

Then came the war. Hunting was greatly curtailed, and maintaining and feeding a pack of hounds became near impossible, so the whole establishment was trimmed down. At the outbreak of hostilities, Ralph was given the heartbreaking job of putting down most of the pack: 'I had to destroy thirty-three couple in two days. I got the hound list and drew them out, one after another, and put them down. It was a terrible thing, and I'd never do it again.'

But under the guidance of Miss B. K. Abbot a nucleus of a pack survived the war, and when the hunt staff returned home from service overseas, she set about the task of restoring, in the words of the motto of the Devon and Somerset Staghounds, 'Prosperity to Staghunting'. Ralph knew the country as well as any man alive, and under the guidance of the old harbourer, Hector Heywood, he had learned the art of tracking and identifying deer. When Hector died, it was natural that Miss Abbot should offer Ralph the job, so in 1945 he commenced the first of his ten seasons as harbourer to the Devon and Somerset Staghounds.

Staghunting is the main sport and recreation of the Exmoor farming community

'The object of harbouring a deer is to find him for the day's hunting. It's your job to find where the deer is. The Master gives you a list of the meets, and you went out the day before to sort out a warrantable stag, a deer that would be right for the hounds to hunt.

'You went on the afternoon before hunting to what you thought was a place where there might be a deer, and perhaps you might meet up with a farmer, a keeper or an estate worker. He would tell you what he had seen in the district and you'd work on from that. There used to be a lot of road-men working on the roads in those days, and as they worked they would tell you if a deer had moved out during the night, and where he had crossed the road.'

Following the various scraps of information given to him by the country people in the area, Ralph would build up a picture of the sort of deer which might be about, all the time looking for signs of a good stag. Eventually, using the evidence of the 'slots', or footprints of the deer, he would endeavour to track a stag to the bracken bed or other cover in which it had lain up for the day.

Those whose acquaintance with wild deer strays little beyond the Christmas card image of Landseer's 'Monarch of the Glen', can only wonder at the information which every little nuance of a deer slot conveys to a man like Ralph Slocombe. From the size, shape and depth of the slot he could tell not just the sex of the deer, but the age, weight and condition, and he could make a fair guess at the configuration of the antlers. A young stag in his first year has only two short spikes on his head, but each successive summer he grows a new pair of antlers with additional points. First he develops his 'rights', the brow, bay and trey points which furnish the lower part of the beam. Then as he reaches maturity, a stag develops additional points at the top of the antler. With 'all his rights and three on top' he becomes a twelve-pointer or royal stag, but frequently a good stag will go on to develop additional points on one or both antlers until, as he gets older, the quality of his head starts to deteriorate with each passing year.

'In the autumn, you always look for the best deer you can find, something with all his rights and three and three or three and two atop. He should always be more than five years old, and you have to tell that by his slot, depending on the soil or where he is walking. If his dew claws print on soft earth then that was pretty well good enough. You knew that he was carrying some venison.'

Using the evidence of his eyes, the harbourer carefully tracks the deer to the place in which he has lain up for the day, and then he tries to catch a glimpse of it. This is where he has to employ all his knowledge and cunning to ensure that he can verify the information which the slots have given him, but without disturbing the stag. Watching from a distance through field glasses, the harbourer might wait until dusk steals down upon the bracken brake, when the deer prepare to spend their night feeding.

The following morning he would need to be up well before dawn, in time to be in a position from which he could watch the stag return to his daytime resting place. In the first ten grey minutes of the new day he would have perhaps his only chance to confirm that there was indeed a warrantable stag in the brake for the hounds when they met maybe six hours later. The stag might shake himself before lying down, giving the harbourer a fleeting opportunity to see him, or perhaps the deer might be spotted by means of a single telltale antler point sticking up above the bracken, necessitating closer investigation.

In Ralph Slocombe's harbouring days, everyone went about their business on the moor by horseback. Farmer, shepherd or harbourer, each would ride to and from their place of work, and so the deer were quite used to seeing horses. Sometimes it was possible to ride slowly past where a stag was lying, just turning the head sufficiently to catch a glimpse of him from the corner of the eye, but not so close that he would catch the scent of the harbourer's horse. For deer have a remarkable scenting ability, and would instantly tell the difference between a hunt horse and one belonging to the local farmer.

Sometimes Ralph used his mare's own intuition to complete his task. Once, in the company of a local farm worker, he had slotted what he knew to be an exceptional stag to a bed of bracken but was then not sure how to get a view of it to finally confirm its location. So leaving his companion watching from behind a tree, he let his horse do the harbouring.

'My old mare, her'd got a sixth sense. I just rode quietly along past where I thought he was laying up, just finger and thumb on the reins, and as we were going along she snorted softly. I just turned my head ever so gently, and there he was, a magnificent stag. I kept quietly riding on, and as soon as I got up on top I just scuttled back to where this farm worker was watching and asked him if he'd seen anything move. "No", he said, so I knew I hadn't disturbed the deer and that he would be there for the hounds.'

It turned out to be the biggest stag of Ralph Slocombe's harbouring career, a seventeen pointer with all his rights and seven and four atop. The antlers hang to this day in Exford village hall.

The harbourer uses every possible trick of woodcraft to find his deer, often watching the reactions of other wild creatures in case they give away some minute clue as to a stag's

RIGHT
The Tiverton Staghounds

whereabouts. On one occasion, after a very poor morning around Dunkery Hill Gate, when it looked as if he might have to admit to the Master that he had found no suitable deer, Ralph spotted two busy magpies in the fork of a dead tree. Every minute or so, one or other of the birds would drop down into the bracken and stay there for a few moments before returning to its perch.

His naturalist's instincts aroused, Ralph stopped to watch the performance from a discreet distance and, looking carefully through his field glasses at the bracken below the tree, saw just the hint of a point, and knew that he had harboured a stag. When he led the huntsman to the place, hounds indeed roused a deer, and when the deer was taken later in

the day, the huntsman noticed that in the crown of one of his antlers there were a few scraps of velvet with maggots in them. He relayed this information back to Ralph. 'I know', he said, 'for that's what the magpies were after'.

Having verified that there is a warrantable stag in the vicinity, it is the harbourer's next duty to report to the Master when the hunt meets at eleven o'clock in the morning. Here, amongst the hubbub of hounds, horses and followers streaming in from the surrounding countryside, he relays the results of his observations to the officials of the hunt and together with the huntsman takes the tufters to find the stag, the one individual stag which he has selected for the chase.

Staghounds, unlike foxhounds, are not taken as a pack in order to rouse their quarry. Instead, a few of the oldest, steadiest and most experienced hounds are selected to act as 'tufters', while the body of the pack is temporarily kennelled at a convenient spot. Taking the tufters to where the harbourer last saw the stag, the huntsman will lay them on the stag's line, from which they will hopefully strike the scent. It is a critical moment for the harbourer, for he has to confirm that once a stag is roused and afoot, it is the one he had in mind. If it is not, the tufters will have to be stopped and taken back to where the chosen animal was harboured. There can be no mistake. A red deer stag is uniquely identifiable by his head, and those who are following the hunt will quickly tell if it is the wrong stag which is hunted out of covert.

As the first burst of music from the tufters echoes about the steep-sided combe, a thrill of excitement ripples through the waiting, watching followers. All around are groups of horsemen and little knots of people craning their necks from the surrounding hilltops, golden in the September morning sun. Deep down in the lanes, crammed between high Devon banks are the car followers, and in a hedgerow gap is a cluster of motorcyclists, their cross-country scramble bikes spattered with mud and dust, their field glasses trained on the wooded valley from which comes the swelling music of the hounds. There are gathered maybe a thousand people in all, each of them eager to spot the hunted stag as he breaks cover. How big is he? What sort of head has he got? Is it that same deer which evaded the hounds last time they were here? Locals confer knowingly, visitors drink in the scene.

The whip gallops round to the far side of the covert, ready to stop the tufters, and at that very moment the deer is away, scattering sheep across the in-bye pastures, cantering up towards the open brown and purple expanse of Exmoor forest. He is a magnificent beast, an autumn stag at the peak of his powers, and as he pauses for a moment on the skyline every head is turned towards him, every pair of field glasses is trained on his russet flanks and mighty antlers. Then he heads once more towards the moor and disappears from view. Down below the huntsman summons the pack and prepares to lay on his full complement of hounds. The mounted field cram down their hats, tighten their girth straps and prepare for a mighty gallop which may take them fifteen miles or more across the moor. Car followers rush for their vehicles and jostle to get out of the lane, motorcyclists kick-start their iron steeds and roar off down some muddy track. For all of them, the day's sport is about to begin – but for the harbourer, his job has ended. Once the pack is laid on, then the responsibility of hunting and accounting for the stag is the huntsman's alone.

A good deal has changed on Exmoor since the late 1940s when Ralph Slocombe was harbouring. The deer were much wilder in those days, for Exmoor itself was a quieter, more remote place. As Ralph comments:

'The moor was less populated at that time, before the tractor came. Everybody rode horses to do their jobs, and horses worked the fields. But then came the tractors and the cars with their headlights that shone at night while the deer were feeding and travelling. I think it is the lights of the cars that have made the deer less shy.'

Lionel Scott agrees. Now retired from farming on Exmoor, Lionel presently harbours deer for the Devon and Somerset Staghounds, concentrating his energies on the eastern half of the country, between Dunkery Hill Gate, Wheddon Cross, Haddon and Anstey. Deer and deer hunting run deep in his veins, for Lionel's uncle was Ned Lang, who harboured for the staghounds between the wars, and it was from Ned that as an inquisitive young boy he learned the skills of following and tracking the deer. The family tradition has been well entrenched, for Lionel's nephew is Maurice Scott, who himself was official harbourer to the Devon and Somerset during the 1970s and who subsequently took over as Joint Master. Lionel agrees with Ralph:

Lionel Scott

'The deer don't take much notice of vehicles now, they've got used to there being more visitors and walkers in the area. I actually harboured a stag once on the side of Dunkery in a clump of gorse just a few feet across. I saw him go in and once he settled down he was perfectly hidden. But the point was that this gorse was inside a corner where two paths met. There were walkers going past him all morning and although none of them ever spotted him, you'd never have believed a stag would've stayed there – but he did!'

The country itself has altered greatly in the last thirty years, and many of the old bracken beds and rough moorland pastures have been brought into cultivation or turned over to improved pasture. Any stretch of land which was reasonably accessible was ploughed up, with the result that today the deer are more exposed on the hills than their forebears. However, there has also been a great deal of forestry planting, and this has provided new blocks of dense cover in which the job of harbouring a deer can be difficult.

Perhaps the biggest change which has overtaken, even revolutionised the craft of the harbourer is the advent of twentieth-century communications, in particular four-wheel-drive transport and the telephone. Lionel uses a short wheelbase Land-Rover to get about the moor, and has the most tremendous admiration for the old timers like Ralph who did the job from horseback.

'How the old harbourers used to do it on a horse I don't know. They had to stay at a farm overnight, and they had maybe a two-hour ride in the morning before it got light in order to get to a place where they could see deer. And then after harbouring a stag they had to look after the horse before getting some breakfast. It's easier in a Land-Rover, but I might still have a fifty-mile round trip out and back in the evening if I'm harbouring across the far side of my country, and the same again the following morning before daybreak. You've got to make sure you start out with a full tank of petrol.'

The statement is made laconically, and one guesses that it comes from bitter experience. He admits that there is a certain disadvantage in his not riding. It is more difficult for him on a hunting morning to show the huntsman exactly where the stag is lying. 'It must be a little inconvenient for Denis, my not riding, but I walk in where I can and help him out, and there are generally local farmers who will do the riding for me.'

The telephone, too has made a big difference to the harbourer's life. Instead of having to visit keepers and farmers at all hours of the day and night, he has merely to pick up the telephone in order to speak to a cottager at some outlying farm miles away across the far side of the country. Lionel will make up to ten telephone calls for each of his meets, just to obtain local information on the movements of deer, for local knowledge is as important to the harbourer as it has ever been.

'You can't work on your own, it's impossible. You've got to have local knowledge, and, most importantly, you've got to know who is reliable.'

Equally, a harbourer has got to know when to keep his own mouth shut. The slightest indication that there's a big stag in a wood close to where hounds are shortly to meet would quickly have every amateur harbourer for miles around combing the area for a glimpse of him, with the inevitable result that by the time hounds meet, the stag will be twenty miles away. But apart from a natural reticence, there are other qualities which characterise a good harbourer. Good eyesight is important – Lionel Scott reckons that for all his years, his own eyesight has improved since he started the job.

'I think that since I've been harbouring and using field glasses more, my eyesight's got keener. I'm sure it has. I can see a stag through the glasses at a fair distance, and I can tell a good stag by the way he walks.'

Just as important is an eye for the country. Skill and patience in woodcraft and slotting is essential, since even today up to a third of the stags may be harboured without the harbourer ever seeing more than their slot marks. The few minutes of grey half-light at around five o'clock in the morning are frequently too short to allow the harbourer a glimpse of his quarry, and so he has to go by other evidence and trust his own judgement.

And a harbourer, like everyone else, needs luck. 'You've got to be in the right spot at the right time. How many do we get by seeing only just a quick flash of them or the tips of a pair of ears in the bracken? You've got to depend on a lot of luck.'

Though he is now retired from the farming life, Lionel Scott thinks of his job of managing the red deer of Exmoor in just the same way as a farmer addresses the business

of managing a dairy herd or a flock of sheep. The weaker beasts must be culled and the better ones left to breed. Numbers must be matched to the carrying capacity of the winter grazing, so the females in particular must be culled to a sensible level. In the course of a season, the Devon and Somerset will take around fifteen spring stags, twenty-five autumn stags and maybe seventy hinds, including road casualties and injured animals.

'You can never take enough hinds, and the season is so short. If you hunt them before November then they might have calves at foot, and if you hunt them too late in March they can be heavy in calf.' It is a dilemma which faces so many who are involved in deer management, and not just on Exmoor. With no natural predators apart from man, the red deer will breed prolifically to the point at which its habitat is no longer able to support it. Then winter can wreak a truly terrible mortality.

Some individual deer may be traced down the years by their progeny. One stag which lived up on Molland Common was harboured eight times by Lionel. Judged a poor specimen, with three and two atop but a small and narrow head, he nevertheless beat hounds on eight occasions, and as far as is known he never was accounted for. Now his descendants survive him, and in Lionel's opinion they too will never make good deer.

'If you look at any animal, perhaps a cow or a ewe, you'll get one that hasn't got as much milk as another. Now her calf or lamb will never do as well as one that's got a good start, and it's just the same with deer. I know there's some deer with twins about this year, because I've seen them myself, sucking the hind. But I doubt whether they'll get as good a start as a single calf. They'll have less chance of making up into a good body, and in a stag, any deficiency will show up in the head.'

The keep on which they are feeding, and even the ground on which they forage for food, has an effect on the quality of the deer. It used to be said that the forest stags from high Exmoor were never as good as the ones from the lower ground around Dunster, for the simple reason that they did not have the benefit of such good feed up amongst the poor vegetation of the barren hills. In addition, the limestone geology of the low country produces soils which are rich in calcium, a mineral which is essential to the development of a strong set of antlers. Nowadays, however, the forest stags develop much better heads because of the amount of moorland which has been reclaimed for agriculture. Where once there was only poor heather and coarse grass to feed on amongst the bracken, today there are succulent crops to raid.

All these things are considerations constantly borne in mind by the harbourer, that constant paradox: a man who loves the deer beyond almost anything else, who lives his life amongst them, studying them, following their movements, watching their courting, their mating and their giving birth, and yet who will ultimately condemn them to the huntsman's gun. He may not like seeing a stag being shot, but he knows that some must die in order that the herd may thrive.

Likewise the hunting farmer of Exmoor has great pride in the deer on his land. He will willingly put up with a certain amount of crop damage and grant a measure of protection to the deer in order that he may enjoy the hunting in its due season. Thus poaching and the killing of deer by unsavoury methods is kept under control; and if so much as a single stag goes missing, then the hunt will quickly get to know about it. Lionel Scott says:

'If there were no hunting, and a farmer had a big herd of deer feeding on his crops, then he wouldn't put up with the damage. He would shoot them, and he would make sure he shot them before somebody else did. But the fact that he loves his hunting, and he spends his holidays coming out for days with the hounds, means that he's prepared to put up with the deer. In fact if it's a good stag, then he's proud to have it on his land when the hunt comes.'

In the old days, when most of the farmers rented their land off one or other of the big estates, there were often clauses written into their tenancy agreements to preserve deer and pheasants. But there were other incentives provided by the hunt itself for the farmers to look upon the deer with a kindly eye. The staghounds maintained a deer fund out of which money was paid to farmers who had suffered damage from the deer. If a field of roots was raided or a hedge destroyed by the nocturnal ravages of the herd, then the Hunt Secretary would pay a visit and come to terms with the farmer. The payout could be as much as £50 in some severe cases, a great deal of money to an Exmoor farmer in the 1930s. A further sweetener came in the shape of a venison handout: whenever a deer was taken, the carcase was jointed and the venison distributed amongst the farmers upon whose land the deer had fed. That tradition remains today.

Nevertheless, poaching does occur from time to time, and produces the most horrible results. Should a wounded deer be found, it is always a matter of the first priority for the hunt to deal with it, no matter how fine a stag the harbourer might have located in some nearby combe. It does not normally take long – a wounded deer does not run far before it is brought to bay and despatched by the huntsman's gun.

Hunting, and especially staghunting, remains as central to the life of Exmoor today as it has been down the centuries. It is the main sport and recreation of the local farming population, and a focus for the life of the community, where news is exchanged, deals are done and friendships renewed. Go to a meet of the staghounds at some small Devon inn, tucked away in a steep-sided valley on the fringe of the moor and the talk will be country talk. Across the low-beamed taproom and around the soot-blackened hearth, aglow with flickering oak logs, the word is of finished cattle averages, of lamb sales, of deer and of hunting. It is the same at the livestock market and at the local agricultural show. When the staghounds took a stand there recently, their display consisted of a collection of the mounted antlers of the previous season's stags. Few exhibits aroused such genuine interest amongst the local people, an indication of the high regard in which the deer are held by Exmoor's hunting farmers.

Village life, too, is bound up with the affairs of the hunt. Not only does hunting provide employment – horses to be shod and fed, visitors to be accommodated and mounted, vehicles to be maintained – but it also provides entertainment. Seven hundred people used to be invited to farmers' lunches before the last war, when sides of beef and barrels of beer were produced by the Masters in an enormous marquee at Exford Horse Show. In earlier times, venison suppers were held by the staghounds at Porlock and at Dulverton Town Hall. Today's entertainments are rather more modest in scale – hunt suppers, whist drives, coffee mornings and bring-and-buy sales – yet in an area where there are no cinemas, theatres or nightclubs, such things are of importance to community life. Despite all the pressures, the enormous increase in the number of summer visitors, the traffic and the changing nature of Exmoor itself, it appears that staghunting retains the support of a majority of the local people. While that state of affairs continues, then there remains a secure future for Exmoor's red deer.

WHERE FLOWS THE CRYSTAL RIVER

Otter hunting was enjoyed by kings and nobles, by gentry and yeomen alike down the centuries. A few men hunted the otter for a living, and less than a handful are alive today. One of these is Tommy Harrison.

Tommy Harrison with the Kendal and District Otter Hounds
RIGHT: The quiet waters amongst the summer meadows

Picture a summer riverbank in the green heart of the English countryside. Wooded hills and broad rolling cornfields, tinged with the first flush of gold, sweep down into the vale. There in the valley bottom lies a network of ancient water meadows, their rich green sward spangled with buttercups and scented with the heady waft of meadowsweet amongst which the fat cattle graze contentedly, swishing the humming flies from their broad backs with a lazy swipe of the tail. Between the meadows lies a network of dykes, lined with willows and alders, beneath whose shade the lush reedmace flourishes and the yellow lilies bloom.

Into this pastoral scene enters a splash of colour, a note of excitement and urgency. Through a distant farm gate beside the winding river comes a figure dressed in a uniform of blue and scarlet and bearing a hunting whip and a long wooden pole. Behind him, a pack of hounds bursts through the gateway and pours excitedly and impatiently across the grass towards the beckoning waters. They are a mixed lot. Tall, dark, shaggy-coated doghounds with noble heads and deep jowls jostle with wise old foxhounds and a little white harrier bitch who darts hither and thither between the reed clumps. And amongst them is the figure of their huntsman, resplendent in his scarlet coat and blue breeches and cap, the twinkling horn protruding from between the brass buttons of his coat, attached to it by a leather thong.

Next comes a bevy of followers. Some of the older ones appear wise and knowledgeable in the blue uniform of the hunt. They walk quietly, exchanging just a few words or a knowing glance between themselves, and watch intently the moving hounds. Others stroll in shirt sleeves, taking in the sweet summer air and enjoying the glory of the scene unfolding around them. A few younger lads and their girlfriends talk animatedly amongst themselves, their minds less on the hounds and more upon each others' company. And from across a hedge beside the lane leans a group of older folk, binoculars in their hands, their cars pulled up on the roadside verge.

The uniformed figure in the lead, a lad in his late teens, now recognisable as the whipper-in, stops a moment, stoops down at the water's edge and picks something up, passing it to the huntsman. A moment later the older, woolly coated hounds dash to the riverbank, their feathered sterns lashing from side to side with excitement, and like a peal of bells, their deep voices sound across the water. With a cheer, the huntsman casts his pack along a side dyke, down which they work with a will until they check at a gnarled and ancient willow; then the old hounds challenge again, hunting a line back towards the river between the purple loosestrife and meadowsweet, their voices ringing with renewed confidence.

For two miles the moving tapestry meanders its way downstream, the hounds hunting out every little patch of waterside cover, every bramble bush and reedy clump, speaking more regularly now, until a sage and battle-scarred old foxhound swims to investigate the hollow roots of a willow into which has washed a tumble of twigs, branches and weedy jetsam. Thrusting his muzzle deep into the hollow bank, he lifts his head and roars a roar which sends a visible bolt of electric excitement through hounds and spectators alike. The pack dives as one into the river, each hound trying to confirm or deny the precious story that their colleague has conveyed to them, together sending up a chorus which makes the valley resound, throwing its echoes as far as the oaks of the hanger that tops the distant hills. Three fields away a couple of thoroughbred hunters out to grass prick up their ears, dancing and snorting with joy as the staccato notes of the beloved hunting horn punctuate their summer slumber.

For a moment all goes quiet. The hounds cast themselves upstream and down, uniformed figures move without bidding to vantage points along the riverbank, some gathered about a gravelly shoal, others where a dyke discharges into the limpid waters of the main river. A farmer with his horn-handled crook, dressed in an old tweed cap and jacket, watches the water around the roots of the willow holt, and even the courting couples stay their amorous conversation and line the reed-fringed water. Then, from far below comes a view holloa, long, strong and confident. Standing up to his knees in the river is the figure of the whipper-in, his pole in one hand, pointing downstream, his whip tied across his chest, his blue cap held aloft. The otter hounds have found their quarry.

The picture is one which was once a regular feature of the rivers, lakes and streams of Britain, from the wide reed-fringed estuaries of East Anglia to the wooded combes of the West Country, from the chalk streams of Hampshire and the verdant vales of the Welsh border country to the broad, rocky rivers of Northumberland and Dumfriesshire or the Cumbrian lakes. Until the otter was placed upon the schedules of the Protection of Plants and Wild Creatures Act throughout England and Wales in 1978 and was granted similar protection in Scotland two years later, those whose first love was hounds and hunting turned in summer to the otter hounds for their sport.

It was a sport with a long and honourable history. Far back in the twelfth century Henry II kept a pack of otter hounds and employed a professional huntsman, one Roger Follo, to look after them. Thereafter otter hunting was enjoyed by kings and nobles, by gentry and yeomen alike down the centuries. Izaac Walton, for example, records a seventeenth century otter hunt at Amwell in Hertfordshire in his *Compleat Angler*. When set alongside eight centuries of otter hunting, the pursuit of the fox is a mere stripling.

Otters were probably first pursued for thoroughly practical reasons. Before the Reformation, the observance of weekly fish days was universal, and since the transport network was unable to convey freshly caught sea fish to anywhere that was more than a mile or two from the coast, most people dined regularly on freshwater fish, such as those caught from the stew ponds alongside every monastic foundation or important dwelling.

An otter in the stew pond was therefore a matter of great concern, and the otter hound the surest and most sensible way of dealing with the problem. It cannot have been long before the hunters recognised that in the otter they had a highly intelligent adversary, against which it was necessary to bring into play venatic skills of the highest order and complexity. And so what was originally a pest control exercise became a sport with its own rules and customs and a unique science and language.

In those far-off times small packs of hounds met early in the morning, before sunrise, in order to intercept the otter as he returned from his nocturnal fishing expeditions. Sometimes a single hound on a leash, a 'limer', was used to track the otter to his resting place or 'holt' before the body of the pack was unkennelled and laid on. Each follower carried a spear or 'grains', a two- or three-pronged weapon with wicked barbs which was

That's when the otter hides up in a drain, but you'll be meeting six hours later. You've got to think when hounds start to hunt the drag – "How long has the sun been shining, has there been any rain?" A light shower will freshen the drag up, but a heavy rain will wash it out. There's such a lot to think about.'

Few men ever reached the revered position of professional huntsman of otter hounds. In most cases this was simply because the Master hunted hounds himself, employing a professional only to look after his hounds in kennels and to carry a whip in the field. When one considers the onerous duties involved in being Master of a pack of hounds of any sort, it is hardly surprising that otter hunters, like beaglers, were often only prepared to shoulder the responsibility of Mastership in return for the rare privilege of carrying the horn themselves.

A good amateur was a delight to behold, and some were very good indeed. For those with a passion for the deeper mysteries of venery, the opportunity to see at close quarters the interplay between a gifted huntsman and his hounds was one of the glories of otter hunting. But an amateur huntsman, by definition, does not depend for his livelihood upon his performance in the field – if he makes an unspectacular fist of hunting hounds, his job is not on the line. For the professional huntsman, however, anything less than excellence is unthinkable, and providing a high quality of sport is not just his pleasure, it is his bread and butter. In otter hunting, where the field had every chance to study at closest quarters the performance of their huntsman, the pressures could be severe. Only the best survived, those who had a complete empathy with their hounds and an intuitive sense when it came to hunting an otter. Tommy makes the job sound deceptively simple:

'You've just got to watch the hounds all the time. With those North Yorkshire hounds, I could tell when there was anything about even if they weren't speaking, just by watching the way they moved. Depending on what you were hunting, sometimes they never spoke at all, especially if it was a bitch otter which carries very little scent. But I knew there was an otter there, just by watching the hounds. You would see them on their toes all the time just looking for something, and you'd see them put their noses down even if they didn't speak to a drag.

'I remember once in Northumberland we were hunting a little beck. There was plenty of water coming downstream and as the hounds went up it they had this look about them. I could tell that there was something about just by watching them, even though not a hound spoke, so I said to the whips "watch out, there's an otter not far away". I think we only went another hundred and fifty yards before we found.

'And coming down the Eden there were always people trying to tell you "there's a drain here and a rabbit hole there", but I'd say no, there's no need to try them, those hounds will tell me where the otter is. And so they did, because eventually the hounds got that look about them and I said "the otter's down in that hole, I bet that's where we'll find it, and I bet you that's a bitch otter". We did, and it was.'

The Kendal and District hunted the waters of north Lancashire, part of north Yorkshire and the lakes and rivers of Cumbria. Here amongst the green valleys of mossy boulders and lichen-cloaked trees, where sparkling streams splash over the rocks between deep, mysterious pools on their way to the lakes, Tommy and his hounds sought their elusive quarry. Amidst the grandeur of the Cumbrian mountains, hunting the reedy margin of Ullswater or climbing through Ulpha Fell to the headwaters of the Duddon they made a magnificent sight, hounds busily examining each rock, root or bankside hollow, while between them strode Tommy, in blue woollen breeches and scarlet coat, his heavy nailed fell boots effortlessly consuming the miles.

'Our best rivers were the Lune and the Eden, but the Hodder was a beautiful river, especially before the war. The Ribble wasn't that good a river for otters in my day, but talk to the old people and it was a different matter. In those days they had a hunt club and invited different packs so many days a year, and they were guaranteed to find a brace of otters every time they went out.'

That was when the Ribblesdale Otter Hunting Association held sway over Lancashire, during the 1930s. The members of the ROHA kept no hounds themselves, but otter hound packs came from far and wide to hunt their country. Regular guests were the Kendal and District, and also the Eastern Counties Otter Hounds which travelled north from their headquarters in East Anglia to hunt the fast flowing rivers which tumble down from the Forest of Bowland. The ECOH paid several visits under the command of their most illustrious Master, Lachlan 'Sandy' Rose. One of the greatest otter hunters of all time, Sandy Rose, was a scion of the famous 'Rose's Lime Juice' family, and also had the distinction of having played football for Tottenham Hotspur. A truly larger-than-life character, Sandy would hunt for a week at a time in the Ribblesdale country during the early 1930s, regularly finding six otters in as many days hunting.

Not only did Sandy Rose bring his hounds, he also brought his supporters. For otter hunting was a sociable sport; one of the highlights of the summer was the traditional 'joint week' during which a visiting pack and its host would take it in turns to hunt. Great crowds turned out at the meets, for invariably the best stretches of water were held in reserve for the occasion, and a high quality of sport was both expected and provided.

In the evenings after hunting had finished, all manner of entertainments were organised. Hunt Balls which maintained at least a veneer of respectability, uproarious hunt suppers upon which formality kept but a tenuous hold, and wild evenings in the local hostelries when the singing, dancing and *après chasse* entertainment lasted well into the wee small hours were the norm on such occasions.

Joint weeks in the Kendal and District country were awaited with particularly keen anticipation during the latter years of otter hunting, for they were arranged to coincide with the week of Rydal Show. Rydal, that Mecca of shows for Cumbrian hunting folk, included classes for otterhounds in its hound show every other year, and on these occasions Lakeland became a natural gathering ground for otter hunters. During Rydal week, Tommy Harrison would hunt the Kendal hounds on three days, alternating with a visiting pack, most notably the Buckinghamshire and Courtenay Tracy Otter Hounds under their brilliant huntsman Jeff Hall.

On the Sunday when there was no hunting, the Kendal and District Otter Hounds held a terrier show in a field beside the hunt kennels at Dallam Towers, complete with horn blowing, whip cracking and hollering contests, and hilarious terrier races to leaven the most serious business of judging the dogs. Naturally, Tommy's cottage beside the kennels was open house for the afternoon.

'I used to enjoy the joint weeks. You'd see everybody, all your friends. It was non-stop hunting every day, and there'd be a film show or hotpot supper at night. We'd have big fields and a lot of support.'

More than a hundred turned out to some meets during a joint week, and they came because they knew the sport would be of the highest calibre. Of course the quality of the hunting depended to a large extent upon the weather and water conditions, but the joint week fields were rarely disappointed. Some of Tommy Harrison's most memorable days with the Kendal and District were during Rydal week, such as the occasion of one classic hunt on Ullswater, perhaps his best, which he remembers in every detail.

'We met at twelve o'clock at the White Lion Inn in Patterdale, and as we went down to the lake to draw, we put off a 24lb dog otter almost straightaway. It was twenty past twelve when we found, and that otter spent most of his time swimming in the lake. The hounds, they took it once across the lake and headed right for one of those little steamers which was on a pleasure tour.

'After cutting right across the bottom of the lake, he went into a chimney at Silver Point, a big rocky place which it was a job to shift him from. One of the visiting hunt staff swam round, while I climbed to the top of the rocks and threw a pole down to him. He rattled the pole in the chimney, and out came the otter.

'That otter then swam three miles up the lake, and the hounds hunted him all the way. The sound? Well, that was marvellous. You could hear it right up the valley at Deepdale, two miles away. Anthony Barker who was a keen hunting man was there, waiting for a Ministry fellow to come and test his cattle. Well, the Ministry man turned up and asked Anthony what the noise was. He said "that's the otter hounds, and that's where I should be, not here with a load of cattle!"'

The following day was Rydal Show, and the beer tent was a-buzz with talk of the great hunt. Tommy was walking on air. Throughout the whole of that four hour and twenty minute epic hunt he had barely touched hounds – and the pack had virtually hunted itself.

It was not always so easy. Often otter hunting called for an immense amount of skill on the part of the huntsman, not to mention physical fitness, especially in the fast flowing rivers of the north of England which were liable to flood at short notice. It was not unusual for hounds to meet and move off in the pouring rain but with the water level no higher than usual, only to find by lunch time that the river was in full spate, with all manner of flotsam and debris careering downstream on the turgid brown current. A heavy flood made scenting very difficult for the hounds, as even if they were lucky enough to mark and find an otter, its scent would be borne rapidly away downstream and dissipated. Flood conditions were sometimes downright dangerous, especially if there were a lot of rocks or boulders in the river against which the hounds might be dashed.

On the other hand a drought would reduce streams and rivers to a trickle and force the otters downstream, away from their regular haunts and onto the bigger waters. If by chance an otter were found on too small a stream, there might not be enough water to afford it a sporting chance to escape. Thus most packs expressly hunted 'weather and water permitting', and cancelled the day's sport in case of drought or flood.

On the slow flowing rivers of the south and east of England, such problems of drought and flood rarely prevented hounds from taking to the field. In these areas, however, there were other considerations which Masters had to bear in mind: as otter hunting took place

LEFT
Billy Scott with the Dumfriesshire Otter Hounds

during the summer months, from April to October, hounds had to avoid nesting game. Where the river flowed through one or more of the big shooting estates, it was often better to change the venue or cancel altogether if there were large numbers of young pheasants or ducklings about, rather than incur the wrath of the keeper and the displeasure of his employer. Likewise, in a livestock country many of the riverside meadows contained valuable hay crops, and large fields of precious mowing grass had to be kept clear to preserve good relations with the farming community.

The blue uniform along the riverbank is no more than a distant memory

Ultimately, however, it was the status of the otter which affected the place of otter hunting as a traditional countryside sport. Otter hunting was, and is, the only recognised field sport to have been brought to an end in recent times, and this was due not to anti-hunting pressure from the animal rights lobby but to the general decline of the otter population throughout much of Great Britain, and the otter's subsequent protection on conservation grounds.

It was in the late 1950s that concern began to be expressed about the otter population, and it was the hunts which first drew attention to the fact that they were suddenly finding fewer otters than before. The speed of the decline in some cases was quite remarkable. In 1960 the Eastern Counties Otter Hounds found 36 otters in 57 days hunting; in the following season, however, they found only 18 in 50 days, and their experience was echoed elsewhere in southern England. Even though the otter population did not fall significantly further once it had reached this new lower level, it was clear that otters were no longer present in many of their old haunts. Tommy Harrison described the situation as he saw it in the north-west of England:

'There were plenty of otters on these rivers when I first came. We'd find thirty-five or thirty-six otters a season. We didn't catch very many, but by the late sixties they were getting hard to find and the mink were on the increase. We never killed more than five a season when I was here and at the end of 1969 we stopped catching otters altogether as a matter of deliberate policy. Instead I just caught all the mink I could.

'I think the mink affected the otters. A mink is active all the time, day and night. He'll go and hunt for a couple of hours and then rest up. After he's rested for an hour or two he'll be out hunting again. I think they competed with the otters, but trapping and shooting of otters also had a lot to do with the decline.'

In the south of England, though, that decline can be ascribed to a number of other reasons. First and foremost, and without a moment's hesitation, comes the destruction of habitat: throughout lowland England, and especially in the breadbasket of East Anglia, marshes were drained and cultivated, coverts and reedbeds laid low and put to the plough;

even saltings, which for centuries had lain untouched by more than the odd fisherman or wildfowler, were embanked, levelled and converted into land capable of yielding ten tonnes of wheat per hectare. The old networks of reedy dykes and winding rivers were cleaned out and straightened to speed the flow of water off the land, and vast new flood protection and land reclamation schemes threw sluices and dams across the mouths of estuaries. For the first time in a thousand years, the tide no longer ebbed and flowed through secret channels amongst the mudbanks where the curlew piped and the silver mullet splashed on a summer's evening.

All this was done in the name of agricultural necessity, an understandable, even laudable aim at a time when the memories of Hitler's U-boats and the spectre of the ration book were seared deep into the nation's consciousness. But the policy of increased food production, fostered and encouraged by successive governments of all hues, was carried out with a ruthless singlemindedness, a determination which swept all before it and which only discovered when it was already too late that it had destroyed something beyond price, sacrificed a treasure which could never be replaced. By then it had ripped the heart out of the wetlands of lowland Britain.

Alongside the rape of the wetlands came the deadly persistent pesticides such as aldrin and dieldrin. Although they were hailed as valuable allies in the fight for increased food production, it was eventually realised that they caused havoc to those creatures, such as the otter, which were at the top of the food chain. The poisons leached off the land and into the waterways, slowly concentrating in the tissues of fish, frog and invertebrate, thence transferring their wicked properties to the hapless otter. The result was sterility and ultimately death. The withdrawal of these chemicals from widespread use came just in time to save some of the more magnificent birds of prey, but by then the otter had already been dealt a terrible blow.

Not all the destruction of our rivers and marshes was in the pursuit of food production. The post-war years saw unprecedented urban and industrial growth, and water meadows over which the otter hounds had hunted between the wars were swallowed up by concrete and asphalt. Great cities spread their tentacles ever further into the countryside, and new towns sprang up where once there had been only quiet and sleepy waterside villages. Each came equipped with its complement of sewage treatment works, and each tapped deep into the ground for the water supplies its inhabitants demanded, slowly but surely sucking the life out of rivers which had once flowed deep, clear and sweet, turning them into fetid stinking ditches, devoid of life and from which thirsty cattle turned in disgust.

Tommy Harrison

This, then, was the relentless tide which sent the otter into a spiral of decline, a spiral which was monitored by the otter hunters with a mixture of despair, resignation and anger. Despair because they saw their sport slipping away, season by season; resignation because they knew that the cause was beyond their control, in the hands of Water Authorities and Ministers of Agriculture. And anger because they were being blamed.

Conservationists and politicians alike cast the otter hunters as the villains of the piece, and perhaps that is hardly surprising. Groups of uniformed men, armed with poles and in command of packs of otter hounds, do not at first sight commend themselves to the casual onlooker as representatives of a movement aimed at the protection of otters. Yet they were dedicated to the conservation of their quarry and in the latter years at least, the number of otters killed by hounds was negligible. Operating through an efficient bush telegraph which drew intelligence both from the activities of the hounds, the fieldcraft of the hunters and from a range of other sources such as gamekeepers and water bailiffs, the hunts kept an accurate assessment of the population and the movement of otters within their areas of operation. On hunting and non-hunting days alike, followers were constantly out on the riverbank, checking for signs of padding or looking under bridges for spraint, information which would help the huntsman decide, when hounds were in the area, where to draw for an otter.

Today, the only surveys of Britain's otter population are carried out by the scientists. Blue uniforms moulder away among mothballs in the attic, photographs of summer hunts along the river fade, as do the memories of those who took part in them. The old otter hounds have long gone to hunt more celestial waters, and their kennels lie deserted.

At Dallam, Tommy Harrison's cottage still remains as it was, but the old Kendal and District kennels have long since been converted into an estate woodyard. Where the old flesh house once stood is now a timber treatment plant, and the hound lodges have been converted into a smart and modern estate office. No more can the singing of the hounds be heard at feeding time – their distant echo is the raucous cacophony of a heronry in the tall trees behind the old kennel yard.

Naturally, Tommy looks back wistfully at the old days:

'I miss the rivers, I miss the music of the hounds and working with hounds in general. I was always out with the hounds. On hunting days we were out along the rivers, but when there was no hunting I always used to be walking out with the hounds down to the water, summer and winter. In the winter of course there was foxhunting, but if it wasn't a foxhunting day then if there was nothing else I could be getting on with, I used to take the hounds out walking for two or three hours.

'Just being with them along the riverbank. I suppose that's what I miss most.'

THE STAG OF THE STUBBLES

If your joy is to watch a pack of hounds puzzling out the line of their quarry, to see them casting back and forth in their endeavours to touch the faintest thread of scent which clings precariously to the frosted stubble, then beagling is for you.

The Bleasdale Beagles

Beagling with the Colchester Garrison

Wilfrid Blunt's 'Old Squire', soliloquising in the twilight of his years at the turn of the nineteenth century, was no fool. He might have been a bit of an old reactionary to knock the new-fangled sport of foxhunting, with all its hooroosh and mad galloping between those wretched new inclosure fences. Such things were for the young bloods, for dashing bucks with more money than sense, with wagers to win and women to impress. Yes, he may have been something of a stick-in-the-mud, but he was no fool. His hunting was a far subtler business altogether, and a far more ancient one.

Even now his view is shared by a small but by no means insignificant section of the hunting community, those who follow harriers and those who hunt with beagles or basset hounds and pursue the hare in the time-honoured and traditional manner. They reckon that from their two feet they see a good deal more hunting than the average horse-powered foxhunter, and on the whole they're probably right. There might not be the prestige or the glory attached to harehunting that is associated with the pursuit of the fox, but there is certainly unparalleled opportunity to absorb and delight in the intricacies and complexities of hound work.

If your joy is to watch a pack of hounds puzzling out the line of their quarry, to see them casting back and forth in their endeavours to touch the faintest thread of scent which clings precariously to the frosted stubble, to hear the burst of music as they run from barren plough to rich-scenting grass, to view the hunted hare stealing away, ears flat, body pressed to the ground while hounds are at fault three fields ahead; if it is your pleasure to attempt to fathom, from the evidence presented by the pack, in what manner the hare has once again escaped – then beagling is for you.

Of course it is not solely the love of hunting's finer details which regularly brings beaglers thronging out into the fields on a winter's afternoon. Some just come for a good walk in the country, unhindered by the legal technicalities of foot-

I like the hunting of the hare
Better than that of the fox;
I like the joyous morning air,
And the crowing of the cocks.

I like the hunting of the hare;
New sports I hold in scorn;
I like to be as my fathers were
In the days ere I was born.
The Old Squire
WILFRID BLUNT

paths and public rights of way, and with a good helping of pageantry and tradition thrown in for good measure. Some come to walk the dog, for dogs are allowed out beagling as well as their owners, provided that they are well-behaved and do not commit the cardinal sin of chasing the hare.

On the whole, however, dog-walking beaglers tend to be the less knowledgeable ones. Like the splendid lady with spaniel in tow who, one bright day over crisp, fresh-fallen snow on which hounds had done precisely nothing for at least two hours, beamed at the huntsman with the immortal words 'Have they seen the fox yet?'

They hadn't, of course, seen *the* fox, nor indeed had they seen *any* fox, for which we whippers-in were duly grateful. Certainly they hadn't seen a hare or even caught wind of one. They did, however, encounter a fine selection of deer later that afternoon, so the lady in question did eventually see a bit of a hunt.

She also saw some wonderful country. That particular encounter took place in deepest Suffolk, in a rolling landscape of high hedges and timber-crowned hills, where the hoar by implication that they were almost guilty of unsporting practice – until it was quietly pointed out by a member of the audience that this was the Association of Masters of *Harriers* and Beagles, and that the official maximum height for a harrier is twenty-one inches. The speaker was a well known Master of Harriers, and wondered if he was held to be guilty of bad sportsmanship.

When hunted as they should be, harriers can provide some thoroughly absorbing sport, and I shall always have a soft spot for the old-fashioned West Country type which used to grace the kennels of the North Norfolk Harriers, the pack with which I first started hunting as a boy. What a shame that these beautiful hounds, with their deep voices and low scenting abilities, are so rarely seen today. Even then, in the late 1960s, there were only two packs still in existence that devoted their energies solely to the hunting of the hare: the North Norfolk and the Wensleydale, the former being hunted from the back of a horse and the latter being hunted on foot. All the traditional West Country packs had long since turned their attention primarily to the hunting of the fox.

Yet one of the very best demonstrations of hare hunting that I have ever seen was given some years ago by the Bolebroke Beagles on one of their annual visits to the moors of Northumberland. Hailing from the gentle countryside of Kent and East Sussex, those little beagles stood no more than fourteen inches high, yet they hunted with the drive and determination of a pack of foxhounds. Quickly finding a hare on the side of a grassy, rush-strewn valley which formed a natural amphitheatre in front of the large and distinguished field, they drove their quarry round in a series of three identical circles until finally they killed, down in the valley bottom. Not once did they check for more than a few seconds, not once did they require assistance from their huntsman, Richard Standring, who nevertheless ran like a stag alongside them; never were they out of sight of the field, who stood spellbound throughout the performance, and they ran so well up together that you could have spread the proverbial tablecloth across them during the entire hunt. At its conclusion, Richard doffed his cap and took hounds back to their van leaving the company speechless with admiration.

Like all other forms of hunting, beagling takes place only with the consent and the goodwill of the local farmers and landowners, and thus a principal job of any Master of beagles is to maintain cordial relations with the farming community. Arranging meets involves checking with the farmers in the district to be hunted and clearing matters with any shooting interests. Beaglers also have an added complication, for the hierarchy of hunting dictates that the foxhounds have first call on any particular piece of country when arranging their fixture list. Thus the Master of beagles, if he shares his country with a pack of foxhounds, has first of all to agree dates with the local MFH.

It's got to be done and it isn't difficult. But it can be frustrating when a Master of beagles is trying to spread the hunting fairly across the country at his disposal, and an MFH decides to be obstructive. One noted MFH required telephoning at six o'clock in the morning, and in order to fix a single beagling meet in his country it would be necessary to have at least half a dozen potential places to go to. The answers would be both predictable and monosyllabic: 'No, no, no, no, no, oh all right'. A telephone call to his neighbouring Master would elicit the reply: 'Well I haven't got round to fixing my meets yet for next month. Tell me where you're going when you've sorted it out, and I'll arrange my meets around you'. He will go far, that man.

Some farmers are happier about beagles than they are about foxhounds. Their reservations normally relate solely to the question of damage, which can be caused by even the best regulated mounted fields when two hundred horsemen and women turn out on a Saturday. Beaglers, operating on foot, leave barely a trace of their passage. On one occasion a Master of beagles had been informed that a certain farmer did not want hounds on his land, and he had therefore carefully shaded off that particular block of land in red on his map, marking it in large capital letters 'NOT ON THIS FARM'.

When the day of the meet arrived, hounds inevitably ran straight onto the forbidden territory, and with a sinking heart, the Master with some difficulty stopped the pack. Having gathered up the last of the stragglers, he was heading back towards friendly country when he saw the farmer approaching. Turning towards him, the Master swept off his cap and said 'I'm terribly sorry, I know you don't want hounds on your land. As you can see, I've stopped them and I'm taking them away'. The farmer replied 'Oh, I don't mind the beagles, it's the blasted foxhounds I don't want'. The beagles hunted that farm from then onwards.

The best huntsman is one who is calm and quiet

Much mystery and legend attaches to the hare, traditional quarry of the beagle. Always referred to by hunters in the feminine or as the enigmatic 'puss', country folk have other names for her, like 'old Sally' or 'old Sarah'. There is even an Old English poem which gives a list of seventy-seven names for the hare – the lurker in ditches, the stag of the stubbles, the dew-hopper, the furze-cat and so on. The list of names formed a spell, an incantation which the hunter was supposed to recite upon setting out for the chase if he wished to have the hare delivered to him. Today's hare hunters put their trust in their hounds rather than wizardry, but down the ages there has been a strong association between the hare and magic or witchcraft. It used to be thought that a witch could transform herself into a hare and vice versa, and there are still superstitious folk who will happily dine off rabbit, pheasant and all manner of other game, but who will yet refuse to eat hare. No serious beagler now believes in the broomstick theory, but it is sometimes quite amazing how a hare can simply vanish in front of hounds for no accountable reason.

In fact a hare can travel a remarkable distance unseen. Even in a field which at first glance looks entirely flat and without cover of any sort, she can find a furrow, a fold in the land, perhaps the line of an old drain, and creep along it for hundreds of yards at considerable speed. The huntsman must then be prepared to start casting in circles around the spot at which she has apparently vanished, and not give up until he is rewarded with success. It is not always easy. After all, a hare is well able to slip away unobserved in situations where a fox would find it impossible to do so.

She will also perform the most remarkable acrobatics in order to give hounds the slip. I alone along a road, with no hounds anywhere in sight to give the game away, a beagler is frequently mistaken for a dismounted horseman. Down winds the car window and out floats the merry quip 'Wot, yer lost yer 'orse, mate?'. Very droll. But perhaps it is not surprising that folks who habitually run around the countryside in riding caps – even if they were designed for hunting long before they were generally adopted by riders – get themselves mistaken for fallen jockeys. The hunting cap is a most unsuitable thing to run about in all day, and those packs which have adopted the far more practical alternative of a soft peaked cap are much to be congratulated.

Even the inconvenience of the hunting cap must be as nothing when compared with the headgear of beaglers of yesteryear. Imagine having to run all afternoon in a top hat, as did the inhabitants of that splendid painting 'The Merry Beaglers', which depicts the Rev Philip James Honywood and his pack at Marks Hall, Essex. Parson Honywood was a noted breeder of beagles and hunted in the same country as do the present-day Colchester

Colonel Easten (*second from left*) on his last day as Master of the Colchester Garrison Beagles

Garrison. In that famous picture, painted in 1847, Honywood and his companions are wearing green jackets, white trousers and tall 'stove-pipe' hats. A silk topper may look splendid atop the head of a mounted foxhunter, but it must be desperately uncomfortable to run in, and is certainly not the thing in which to squeeze through a smallish gap in a blackthorn hedge. A hunting cap seems positively *avant garde* by comparison.

Apart from the cap, the beagler's hunt livery is really rather practical, provided you don't mind washing your breeches after each and every day in the field. It is warm, comfortable and weatherproof, and lends a timeless quality to a day's hunting. I well recall hunting one February on the edge of the Cotswolds, just as lambing was getting into full swing. It was quite late in the afternoon, most of the small

midweek field had gone home, and I was alone with hounds towards the end of a hunt. The pack was half a field ahead, pressing on across a piece of old pasture, down the side of a dry stone wall and through a gateway by an isolated, tumbledown barn which stood far out in the fields, miles from the nearest farmstead.

I arrived breathless at the gateway, horn in hand, looking to see which route hounds had taken, and found that beside the barn and its small stockyard was a shepherd. He was lambing down his ewes in the barn, and had them penned in wooden hurdles situated around the outside of the ancient, ivy-clad stonework. He was dressed in a brown cotton smock and hessian gaiters, he wore an old felt hat and his cheeks were the colour of a Cox's orange pippin.

It could have been a tableau from the last century. As the shepherd signalled the direction in which he had seen the hare disappear, I felt that the whole scene could have been lifted from some old sporting print. It was almost as though, for perhaps half a minute, I had wandered into a time warp; me in my neo-Victorian costume and he in his rustic workaday garb. Nobody else who was out hunting saw that shepherd and I never came across him again, but the picture is still vivid in my mind and I shall always remember the encounter.

A rather more incongruous sartorial juxtaposition was that which I once contrived with a group of ramblers. Hounds were running some three or four fields away in the bottom of a valley, and I was doing my best to catch up with them. Running downhill towards a thick, tall hedge, which I had to cross in order to get nearer to my objective, I spotted a five-barred gate. Taking a run at it, I leaped onto the topmost rail, caught my foot and crashed to the ground on the far side, measuring my length in the mud. As I blinked and looked up, there standing over me, staring incredulously at this antique-garbed apparition which had literally hurled itself into their midst, was a happy party of hikers, spotless in their blue and red kagoules. As I picked myself up, their jaws dropped in wonder and amazement. So I raised my cap, bade them good afternoon and ran on my way. To this day I don't know which party was the more startled, them or me.

There has been a good deal of concern expressed recently in some quarters about the apparent decline in the hare population. Much of it has come from the shooting fraternity, who have looked back over their estate bag records and found that the number of hares shot has, over the years, fallen markedly in some areas. Naturally, any fluctuation in the hare population is a matter of considerable interest to hare hunters, and the Association of Masters of Harriers and Beagles has for some years been monitoring the number of hares found by packs of hare hounds in various parts of the country. It has thus been provided with information which helps to build up a picture of the dynamics of hare populations.

Hare numbers are known to fluctuate quite widely, and any beagler will tell of parts of his hunting country in which hares will be quite literally swarming, and others in which he will have to search hard to find even one. Quite often such areas will be just a few miles, or maybe only a few fields apart from each other, but why hares should be so hard to find in some areas is difficult to answer. It may well have something to do with the increasing popularity of lurchers and long-dogs, some of whose owners appear quite content to course their dogs illegally across anybody's land by day or night without permission.

Colonel Easten suggests that the decline, where it has occurred, is related closely to the changes which have taken place in agriculture over the last twenty years, but does not believe that there are any fewer hares in his own part of the country than there were when he started hunting.

'In this part of England we're fortunate; we still have plenty of hares in our country, and the idea of a general population decline is not borne out here. Certainly hares move about, but taken by and large, there are just about the same number as there were twenty years ago.'

He has, however, witnessed many changes to the sport of beagling, changes which are common to all hunting in the more populated areas of south-east England.

'Clearing meets has become more and more difficult, and this is bound to continue as the countryside becomes increasingly developed. We ourselves lost meets when the Colchester bypass was opened, and the same thing happened when the new Braintree road was built. The problem is at its worst near the big cities.

'I don't think that it will stop hunting, but it is bound to restrict hunting in certain areas, and more amalgamations will take place. One day we ourselves may have to get together with another pack which is also affected, and make the best of what remains of our two countries.'

Not every change in beagling has been for the worse, however, and one major development has been the democratisation of hunting that has gone hand in hand with the easing of some of the stuffier attitudes of those who follow hounds.

'When I first started beagling, it was very much a middle class – perhaps slightly upper-middle-class – sport. People dressed smartly in tweeds, the men wearing plus twos and stocks and the ladies wearing skirts. They presented the image of being the rather more affluent members of society. Not *the* affluent members of society, of course, because they went foxhunting.

'Over the last twenty or thirty years this has changed. Masters have been very sensible not to worry too much about what people wear to come out beagling, and dress doesn't come into it any more. Today, people feel that they can just come straight from their house or their garden and follow the beagles.

'This has led to hunting becoming accessible to a very much wider range of individuals than before. We have all sorts of people who come out with our hounds: dockers from Harwich, bankers, an engineer on one of the cross-channel ferries, farm workers, a lorry driver, a couple of solicitors, retired army officers, a car dealer, chaps who have got rich quick, chaps who have got poor quick, all of them come out beagling. I'm sure that it is an excellent thing that so many different kinds of people can mix happily together, all united by a common love of beagling.'

Following beagles on foot thus remains one of the least expensive and certainly one of the most accessible of all field sports, a gateway through which countless people have entered the hunting field. The ninety existing hunts are spread far and wide across Britain, providing a ready opportunity to most to get out hunting within thirty miles or so of their home, an opportunity that requires no horses or skills in equitation, no fancy clothes at fancy prices, just a pair of trainers or – if you must – wellingtons, two stout legs and a predilection for fresh air and attractive countryside. There are considerably worse ways in which to spend a Saturday afternoon than with a pack of beagles.

COPPER AND SCARLET

With his scarlet coat gleaming in the low morning sunshine, his buttons polished till they sparkle, his boots burnished like mirrors, the huntsman cuts a fine figure: smart, confident, quietly professional. Now retired from the Whaddon Chase, Albert Buckle served forty-three years in hunt service.

The Essex and Suffolk Foxhounds, c1910

On the first Saturday in November a buzz of excitement runs through the village. Horsemen and women gather outside the pub; riders attired in scarlet and black, smartly turned out on glowing bays and chestnuts with tails combed and manes plaited. Children trot up brightly on small ponies as knots of locals greet and gossip, and from all directions come riders, trailers and lorries – and very soon the roadside verges are crammed with cars, too. Ramps are lowered and horses clatter out onto the gravel as a barmaid busies herself, dodging between the jostling horses to hand round drinks to those gathered in the pub forecourt.

Then all heads turn as around a bend in the lane sweep the hounds – a moving carpet of black, white and tan, with sterns waving gaily they trot eagerly forwards, at their head the whipper-in and amongst them the figure of the huntsman. With his scarlet coat gleaming in the low morning sunshine, his buttons polished till they sparkle, his boots burnished like mirrors, he cuts a fine figure: smart, confident, quietly professional.

It is a proud moment for a huntsman at the opening meet. Here amidst the pageantry of the chase, set in a scene that has graced a thousand chocolate boxes and countless Christmas cards, there is both anticipation and fulfilment. Ahead lies a new season, with all the promise and uncertainty which gives to hunting its spice, its challenge and fascination; behind lie the months of hard work which have brought his pack of hounds to the peak of physical fitness and mental attunement, hour after hour of careful feeding and exercise. Rearing the puppies, tending the lame, sick and injured, visiting farms and collecting fallen stock, skinning, jointing and preparing the food; all these things and many more lie behind those few moments of a huntsman's glory. Before he ever gets near to hunting hounds he must be vet, stockman, butcher, ambassador and a competent horseman into the bargain, and there is a long apprenticeship to be served if he wishes to carry that coveted badge of office, the polished copper horn which peeps from between the third and fourth buttons of a scarlet coat. No wonder the professional huntsman is held in respect and esteem by country people, no wonder that amongst each succeeding generation there are still country boys who long to wear scarlet and carry a hunting horn.

One such lad was the youthful Albert Buckle. Now retired after forty-three years in hunt service, the last twenty-nine of which were served with one pack, the Whaddon Chase, Albert was brought up between the wars in Bicester, then a small Oxfordshire market town. There was nothing he wanted more than to enter hunt service, though his father had other ideas. With a family butcher's business and a small farm to run, he apprenticed young Albert into the butcher's trade, but as Albert himself says:

'I did three years and hated the job. I was obviously no good at it, so eventually he fetched me away, and let me take up a job at the Bicester hunt kennels at Stratton Audley, riding second horse to the second whipper-in.'

It was 1934, and in those days a fashionable pack of foxhounds could expect to employ what by modern standards would be considered an enormous staff. There are few hunts now who employ even a professional second whipper-in, let alone a second whipper-in's second horseman, whose job was simply to ensure that the spare horse was fresh and readily available for the afternoon's sport. But from the Stratton Audley kennels in the

RIGHT
The North Cotswold Foxhounds at Guiting Power

1930s there were seven men in scarlet coats who rode out on a hunting morning – the huntsman, his first and second whips, their three second horsemen and the Master's second horseman. This was before the days of motorised hound vans, and the hunt staff hacked to most of the meets from the kennels, setting out early in the morning and riding up to twelve miles before the day's hunting had even started. As Albert recalls:

'The only place that we used to box to was the country north of Banbury. To get there we had a special train from Bicester station which used to run on hunting mornings. We would hack to Bicester and load the hounds and horses into a railway waggon that took us to Woodford Halt, which was pretty central to the Saturday country. We unboxed there, hunted all day and then took the train back to Bicester at night before hacking home.'

Such an arrangement was by no means uncommon in the countryside between the wars, when the rural branch line was still a feature of village life, and many hunts relied upon the railways to transport both horses, hounds and followers to and from their meets.

Albert Buckle. RIGHT: The Boxing Day Meet of the South Devon Hunt

It was a hard life for a young man in hunt kennels. The working day started at six o'clock in the morning, and hounds hunted four days a week.

On non-hunting days hounds were walked out before breakfast and then again for two hours or so in the afternoon. All the flesh had to be cooked and the puddings had to be prepared in order to feed the hounds, and of course the lodges, runs and yards had to be kept spotlessly clean – all under the watchful eye of the huntsman.

'They were real shockers, were the old huntsmen in those days. You daren't answer back or anything like that. Out hunting they were always at you, and everything you did had to be quick and sharp. If the huntsman lost a fox it was always your fault, and there were many times I came home and cried at night when the huntsman was at me all day long. It was really hard work and sometimes you used to wonder if it was worth going on. But then you had your hunting and although it was a hard life, it was a good one.'

The turning point for Albert came after two seasons with the Bicester, when he was promoted to the post of second horseman to the huntsman. As such he had the privilege of deputising for the whippers-in when they were off sick, so for the first time he had the opportunity to play a small part in the management of a pack of hounds in the hunting field. It was one step up the ladder of hunt service, though it would still be many years before he could expect to hunt a pack of hounds himself.

'You were expected to serve a long apprenticeship in those days. You didn't even think of applying for a huntsman's job until you'd whipped in for about twelve years. If you did, then as soon as whoever you'd applied to phoned up your own huntsman for a reference, he would get the answer "He's not ready yet". So your huntsman controlled you.

'But there really is a lot to learn if you are going to do a huntsman's job properly. I think that one of the troubles today is that young fellows get on too quickly, and because of that they don't last.'

A hunt servant would expect to move to positions with several different packs before finally landing a huntsman's job. Albert himself left the Bicester after war broke out and served in the army for six years. When he returned from military service in France and Germany he went first to the Hertfordshire, then moved up to Scotland as first whipper-in to the Duke of Buccleuch's hunt, then in 1950 to the North Cotswold. It was there, eighteen years after entering hunt service, that he at last carried the horn and it was a proud day, that first morning at the start of the 1952 season:

'It's a great thrill to be a huntsman. When you start out, riding second horse and working your way up the ladder, that's what you are always hoping to achieve, that's the goal in front of you. I remember when I hunted the North Cotswold for the first time, and it was a great thrill. You get all keyed up, you blow your horn too much and you hope everything goes all right. But you learn by experience. We had a marvellous pack of hounds at the North Cotswold, it was a lovely country in those days and we had a tremendous lot of sport. I thoroughly enjoyed it.'

Then in 1954, Albert Buckle moved to the Whaddon Chase in Buckinghamshire as huntsman to that great figure of the equestrian world, Dorian Williams. Although a devoted Master of Foxhounds, Dorian Williams was an extremely busy man, and so it fell to Albert to do much of the work of running the hunt country and clearing meets with the farmers. It was also Albert's privilege to be allowed to take charge of the hound breeding, something which he considered a great honour.

England was a wonderful place for the foxhunter when Albert Buckle was a young man. Hounds could run all day without ever touching a ploughed field, and even where the land was under arable cultivation, most of the farm work was done by horses and there were very few tractors to spread diesel fumes across the countryside.

'There were no artificial fertilisers on the land to ruin the scenting and very few cars. In the thirties when I was with the Bicester there was hardly any wire at all, and what there was had been flagged by the Hunt Secretary, Colonel Blacker. You could go anywhere across country without even looking; you could take your own line without any fear that you were going into wire. Everything was in your favour in those days and there was really nothing to stop you.'

Even in the 1950s when Albert moved to the Whaddon Chase, the country was little short of heaven to a huntsman, with plenty of foxes, plenty of grass to provide excellent scenting, and little in the way of restrictions. Most of the country was owned by just four or five big estates and nearly all the farms were tenanted, and it was a condition of most of the agricultural tenancies that the farmers had to assist the hounds at all times and remove their wire before the hunt came. That made life much easier for a huntsman and much more exciting for the field, who rode hard at the big hedges and ditches for which the Whaddon country was famous. But it did mean that the hunt staff had to be mounted on the best horses available.

'A huntsman has got to have a good horse. It's false economy to mount him on cheap horses because a horse to a huntsman is a means of conveyance. He can't always be worrying whether his horse is going to get across the next fence, because if he starts looking for gates he will be wasting time. You must always be concentrating on your hounds, not on your horse. I was very fortunate, because Dorian Williams mounted me exceptionally well and I had some marvellous horses.'

Nevertheless, any professional huntsman must expect to take a fall every now and again, for foxhunting is not a sport for the faint-hearted, and Albert took his share – though he considers himself fortunate in that he rarely broke anything more important than his ribs. Sometimes, however, a fall is a far more serious matter, and deaths or crippling injuries do occur in the hunting field.

Yet hunting falls also have their lighter side. One professional huntsman was in the habit of keeping the tips which members of the field gave him on Boxing Day in his hunting boots, and one year he left for the first draw with a veritable bootful of fivers. All went well until he had a crashing fall in which his boot split and its valuable contents were deposited in the bottom of an evil-smelling ditch. So forsaking both his hounds and his loose horse he immediately set about retrieving the sodden banknotes. Upon seeing the muddied and bedraggled figure upon all fours, grovelling about in the undergrowth, his whipper-in rode up, fearing that some terrible injury had been sustained. He leapt off his horse to render medical assistance, only to be handed the horn and told to get on with the job of hunting hounds for the next ten minutes while more important financial matters were attended to.

Even with the boldest and most surefooted horse and the handiest and most biddable pack of hounds, a lot depends upon the huntsman: it is he who injects that spark, that flash of brilliance which can turn a moderate day's hunting into a good one, or a good day into a memorable one. They say that a good huntsman is born, not made, that it is not merely the patient and logical application of hunting science which kills foxes but the mental thread which ties a huntsman to his hounds, so that he only has to think of a cast and his pack flies to the spot. But he must also have a mind like a fox, and use cunning to beat cunning.

'A huntsman has got to be quick. A fox is always trying to get away from you and it's no good your hanging about. When you're cast-

The VWH Foxhounds in kennels at Meysey Hampton

ing you've got to make your mind up quickly, and you want a rough idea in your head as to which way you think the fox has gone. Keep your eyes on your hounds all the time, because there's always an old hound or two that will go on, and then look back at you as if to say "I can't tell you for sure he's gone this way, but I think he has".

'We had an old doghound called Crofter who was like that. One Boxing Day we had a nice hunt down by our point-to-point course, and at the critical moment hounds checked on a road. I let them drift down the road in front of me and this old dog started swinging his stern. Although he didn't say a word, I thought he must have it, and I let him go on. Eventually he came to a crossroads, shot into a gate, threw his tongue and away they went.

'I don't hold with this charging back all the time at a check. I know that you've got to make good your ground, but foxhunting is different to beagling. A hare will dodge back, but a good fox will always want to go on, so when foxhounds check, say in a field that's been foiled by stock, you've always got to take them round the far side of the foil first and try to hit the line off where you think the fox has gone out of the field.'

A significant difference between hunting today and hunting forty years ago lies in the number of epic chases of ten, fifteen or even twenty miles which a hard riding field could have expected before or just after the last war. Of course things are more difficult for the present generation of huntsmen in that scenting conditions on the whole are far worse than they once were, and hunting countries are now hedged about with busy roads and urban development. Nevertheless, a good deal of the deterioration in the quality of sport lies, according to Albert Buckle, in the lack of attention which nowadays is given to earth stopping. The fox is a nocturnal feeder and will normally be abroad at night, and at dawn he will return to his earth to lie up for the day. If access to his home is barred by the earth stopper, then he will make alternative sleeping arrangements, normally lying up in a close and conveniently situated patch of cover. Under these circumstances hounds can readily rouse him and, assuming that all the earths round about have been similarly stopped, they can expect a good run.

'A fox will try all the earths in his area, he might try them twice, and then he will go. That's when you get your long hunt, that's when he goes straight, when he's off his beat. When I was with the Bicester we never took a terrier because we never ran a fox to ground. In those days the old earth stoppers went round at ten o'clock at night with a spade and a lantern. Today they stop in the morning, and half the time they stop the foxes in. Of course you've got to look at the earths in the morning before hunting, to see that an old badger hasn't opened them up again. But the stopping must be done at night when the foxes are out. A lot of these long points they get today, they're really changing foxes several times.'

The fox is renowned for his cunning, and for the tricks he will get up to in order to evade the hounds; for example an old fox may push a young one up in front of him to lead the pack off his own line. Unless the huntsman is right on the spot to see it happen and to stop hounds and hold them onto the correct line, nobody is any the wiser. A fox will also deliberately seek to disguise his scent by running amongst sheep or cattle, or by rolling in a muck heap. He will also know just as well as the hounds which country will carry the poorest scent, and often he will run a road in an attempt to make good his escape. Once, when he was out with the Duke of Buccleuch's hounds, Albert Buckle even saw a fox run along the top of a dry stone wall for nearly half a mile.

A question to which every huntsman must address himself is that of the extent to which he must be a killer of foxes as against a provider of sport for the mounted field. There is little doubt that in its traditional heartlands, foxhunting has helped to maintain a healthy and stable population of foxes, and there the emphasis is placed on maintaining that balance rather than killing every fox regardless of the circumstances. The main business of fox control is carried out during the autumn, when cubhunting splits up the litters and gets the fox population down to a manageable level. Thereafter the hunt has to ensure that farmers and gamekeepers are kept happy and that foxes are seen to be killed; but it is equally important for a huntsman to ensure that a large, eager November field has a fast and exciting day with lots of galloping and jumping, and that long draws in blank coverts or boring sojourns outside deep and cavernous earths are kept to a minimum. For Albert Buckle, the question of whether or not to kill a fox that had been run to ground rested largely on the wishes of the farmer.

'For the hounds' sake the huntsman always wants to kill his fox, because if they've hunted well and put themselves right then they deserve it. But as a huntsman you're also a professional performer, a professional provider of sport. That's what you're there for, that's what the people are paying the money for, and it's sport that you've got to provide for them, or try to.'

Throughout its long history, hunting has had to cope with changes in the countryside, to adapt to new methods of farming and alterations in the pattern of land ownership and to roads, railways and industry. But in the last thirty-six years, since Albert Buckle came to the Whaddon Chase, those changes have been faster and further reaching than ever before, and the English Midlands have been amongst those places which have suffered most severely. Standing on the high ground between Stewkley and Leighton Buzzard as evening casts its veil over north Buckinghamshire, you can look out across what was once some of the finest of the Whaddon Chase country. Even in the fifties, little more than a few twinkling lights from distant villages and the odd isolated cottage would have been seen between the dark shadows of field and covert, the stillness of winter broken only by the barking of a farm dog, the raucous cawing of the rooks and the sound of cattle going in for their evening milking. Look at it now. Bletchley and Milton Keynes sprawl across the landscape, burning with a myriad points of sodium vapour, lighting up the sky with a garish yellow glow. To the north-east winds the A5 and beyond it the M1, luminescent yellow ribbons twinkling with the headlights of speeding traffic, and all about can be heard the sullen roar of civilisation, the subdued growl of the internal combustion engine.

Farming, too, has changed. Where once there were small, neat fields of grass hedged with blackthorn, all is now down to plough, and what grazing remains is no longer the old-fashioned permanent grassland but rotational leys, bounded by electric fencing and dressed with artificial fertilisers. No longer can horse and hound run and jump virtually unhindered. In the 1950s hounds hunted five days a fortnight around these parts, but that

was soon cut down to two days a week and today it would be impossible to find sufficient country to do even that. Like other hunts in similar circumstances, the Whaddon Chase amalgamated with a neighbouring pack, the Bicester, and this arrangement has gone exceptionally well; the combined hunt countries now support four days hunting a week throughout the season, one or perhaps two of which are in the former Whaddon territory.

The problem of finding sufficient space in which to hunt derives not only from the loss of countryside to roads, motorways and urban development but also in no small measure from the growth of shooting. The story is not confined to any one pack and I hear almost identical worries from hunting friends up and down the country, worries which seem to grow more acute with every passing season. Before Christmas it is now difficult to find somewhere for hounds to meet, for everywhere the pheasant is king and the risk of hounds disturbing a covert is more than keepers or shoot owners are prepared to bear.

One well known south of England pack of foxhounds has been reduced from four days a week to barely three, purely because of the pressure from shooting interests. Another has dropped from three days to two, and hounds must be hacked for anything up to four miles from their traditional meets to the first available covert; more and more have to struggle every week to find sufficient country to hunt. One friend from Shropshire described his hunt country as a jigsaw puzzle with half the pieces missing, while another from the Home Counties told me that his Hunt Secretary now has to obtain leave from more than two hundred individual shoots.

Elsewhere areas which once were the finest of hunting countries are now totally devoid of foxes, all of which have been wiped out in the name of game preservation. One huntsman of my acquaintance was welcomed to a regular cubhunting meet recently with the words that he might just as well kill all the foxes he liked because the keeper would deal with any that he missed. What chance there of finding a November fox? Over the years, Albert Buckle has seen the problem grow in the Whaddon Chase country:

'Everybody wants to shoot today, and the keepers have got to provide the birds for them. That's their job. But I don't think they need to destroy the foxes in the way that they do. If they know their trade, they can keep both foxes and pheasants. I don't really blame the keepers so much as the shoot owners. After all, they're the ones who are paying the keepers' wages and they're in a position to tell the keepers what to do. The trouble is that they don't, and when the hounds have a blank day or can't draw a particular piece of country because of the shooting, people blame the keeper.'

One can also well understand the position of the shoot owner, especially if he is committed to providing several expensive commercial days during November and December. When there is a lot of money at stake and when complicated arrangements have to be made in order to provide a series of shooting days, then the potential disruption of a pack of foxhounds hunting through his coverts is one problem the owner can well do without. Nor is it lost upon him that the shooter often pays far more dearly for his sporting rights than the hunter. It is therefore far easier for the shoot owner simply to refuse leave to the hunt and to instruct his keeper to do away with all the foxes.

Yet I find the present state of affairs deeply worrying and disturbing. As someone with a

LEFT
The Pytchley Hounds at exercise

commitment to both hound and gun it concerns me that a field sport of proud and ancient lineage is slowly being squeezed from the face of the English landscape. Where the combined weight of roads, railways, agricultural change and the suburbanisation of the countryside has failed to stifle the hunt, now in some areas at least the pheasant is succeeding. Of course mistakes *can* occur. Hounds *do* run through release pens from time to time, and they can even turn up during the middle of a drive, something which happened once to an MFH friend of mine in Devon. When hounds, after a four mile run, raced between the legs of guns and beaters and the shoot owner turned apoplectic with rage, my friend could do little more than proffer his abject apologies and round up the pack as best he could; thankfully within a few days the two were able to share a good laugh about the incident. On the other hand I have seen hounds strung up in fox wires and others writhing in mortal agony having taken poison illegally administered by gamekeepers.

But such mistakes should not be allowed to do lasting damage, and shooting and hunting should surely be able to coexist peaceably in our crowded countryside. After all, there are many parallels between the two sports. Leaving aside any equestrian motives, the majority of people who go hunting or shooting simply value the opportunity to get out into the countryside and absorb themselves in an age-old craft which either involves them in pitting their own wits against those of a wild creature or in watching someone else do so. At the root of hunting is the fascination of looking at a pack of hounds at work, and of seeing the interplay between a huntsman and a group of working dogs, bred to their task over generations; just as in the same way the very best sport with the gun is – though this is my own opinion – to be found out roughshooting or wildfowling where dog work and hunting skills rather than proficiency with the gun make the difference between success and failure. To the roughshooter or wildfowler, accurate marksmanship is merely the final phase in a hunting operation which has located and flushed his quarry or placed him within range of its flight line.

Hunting, though, is the more social sport. Indeed, one of its great strengths is its ability to bind together the rural community, and traditionally it has provided a focus for country people to meet and exchange news and gossip during the quiet winter months. Although that may no longer be a requirement in the more suburbanised parts of lowland England, there are still large areas of the remoter countryside where foxhunting plays a central part in the life of the community, where social activities such as barn dances, suppers, bring-and-buy sales, coffee mornings and whist drives are all organised by or for the local hunt.

Hunting is an activity which all ages and types of people can participate in and enjoy, as the crowds who turn out to the Boxing Day meets at market squares all over the country amply demonstrate. But at a more local, more personal level, hunting provides a gateway into the countryside; not just the countryside of fields, coverts, hills and hedges – for sure, hunting provides the opportunity to gain access to those – but also the human countryside, the farming families, the farmworkers and village tradesmen who make rural Britain tick.

This was something which first struck me when, as an undergraduate, I used to cycle out for early mornings cubhunting with the Bicester foxhounds. Down in the quiet, dewy fields and misty lanes, around Merton, Ambrosden, Blackthorn and Marsh Gibbon, where hounds met in the first grey flush of an early October dawn, a complete stranger might be welcomed into the lives of local people who shared no more than a love of country matters, of hounds and of hunting. After a busy morning bustling about the coverts, with the warm sun now climbing into the sky, scent disappearing by the minute and hounds hacking homeward along a dusty lane, it would be back to some farmhouse kitchen for a breakfast of home-cured bacon, eggs gathered straight from the hen run, a pocketful of field mushrooms, newly baked bread and farmhouse butter. There was welcome, warmth, and hospitality.

And later, when December's rain and frost had laid bare the land, when north Oxfordshire lay misty under the rose pink light of late afternoon and water lay in the ditches, when hounds hit off the line of their hunted fox with a crash of music from the hills over by Horton cum Studley and galloped down onto Otmoor with a roar that made the hair on the back of my neck stand on end and sent a thrill down my spine, I was among friends. Finally, as evening fell and hounds and hunt staff turned to hack home, tired, wet and mud-spattered, splashing through puddled lanes in which were reflected the last shreds of day from the western sky, ragged and bloodshot, there was a generous sincerity in the farewells.

Foxhunting still enjoys a strong groundswell of support from the rural community, and although mounted fields are now often limited in order to keep damage to farmland to a minimum, these days there are probably more followers out with the Bicester and Whaddon Chase – mounted, on foot, in cars, on bicycles and motorbikes – than ever before. Meanwhile, each children's meet in the Christmas school holidays brings a new generation into touch with hunting, and today there are many children in the countryside and suburbs alike with ponies. In spite of the political opposition which hunting faces, and has continued to face since the 1920s, it all bodes well for the years to come – and Albert Buckle agrees. Although he reckons that he saw the best of foxhunting in the 1930s, he still believes that the sport has a future:

'Hunting is certainly more difficult now than ever it was, and I'm glad I started when I did. Without any doubt the best hunting was between the two world wars, and especially in the 1930s. Day after day you'd have a hunt of an hour or an hour and a half, change horses and have another hour and twenty minutes or two hours. Well it's not like that today, but I still think hunting will keep going on. We all hark back to our memories, but you've got to think of the future and help as best you can. You've just got to make the best of it.'

INDEX

RIGHT
Watching hounds